The Educator's Guide to Action Research

SPECIAL EDUCATION LAW, POLICY, AND PRACTICE

Series Editors

Mitchell L. Yell, PhD, University of South Carolina
David F. Bateman, PhD, American Institutes for Research

The *Special Education Law, Policy, and Practice* series highlights current trends and legal issues in the education of students with disabilities. The books in this series link legal requirements with evidence-based instruction and highlight practical applications for working with students with disabilities. The titles in the *Special Education Law, Policy, and Practice* series are designed not only to be required textbooks for general education and special education preservice teacher education programs but are also designed for practicing teachers, education administrators, principals, school counselors, school psychologists, parents, and others interested in improving the lives of students with disabilities. The *Special Education Law, Policy, and Practice* series is committed to research-based practices working to provide appropriate and meaningful educational programming for students with disabilities and their families.

Titles in Series

Developing Educationally Meaningful and Legally Sound IEPs by Mitchell L. Yell, David F. Bateman, and James G. Shriner

Sexuality Education for Students with Disabilities by Thomas C. Gibbon, Elizabeth A. Harkins Monaco, and David F. Bateman

Creating Positive Elementary Classrooms: Preventing Behavior Challenges to Promote Learning by Stephen W. Smith and Mitchell L. Yell

Service Animals in Schools: Legal, Educational, Administrative, and Strategic Handling Aspects by Anne O. Papalia, Kathy B. Ewoldt, and David F. Bateman

Evidence-Based Practices for Supporting Individuals with Autism Spectrum Disorder edited by Laura C. Chezan, Katie Wolfe, and Erik Drasgow

Special Education Law Annual Review 2021 by David F. Bateman, Mitchell L. Yell, and Kevin P. Brady

Dispute Resolution Under the IDEA: Understanding, Avoiding, and Managing Special Education Disputes by David F. Bateman, Mitchell L. Yell, and Jonas Dorego

Advocating for the Common Good: People, Politics, Process, and Policy on Capitol Hill by Jane E. West

Related Services in Special Education: Working Together as a Team by Lisa Goran and David F. Bateman

The Essentials of Special Education Advocacy by Andrew M. Markelz, Sarah A. Nagro, Kevin Monnin, and David F. Bateman

Disability and Motor Behavior: A Handbook of Research by Ali S. Brian and Pamela S. Haibach-Beach

Supporting and Accommodating Students with Special Health Care Needs by Azure D. S. Angelov and Mary Jo Rattermann

You're Hired! Practical Strategies for Guiding Individuals with Autism Spectrum Disorder to Competitive Employment by Patricia S. Arter, Tammy B. H. Brown, and Jennifer Barna

Unraveling Dyslexia: A Guide for Teachers and Families by Kristin L. Sayeski

Disability, Intersectionality, and Belonging in Special Education: Socioculturally Sustaining Practices by Elizabeth A. Harkins Monaco, L. Lynn Stansberry Brusnahan, Marcus Charles Fuller, and Martin Odima Jr.

The Educator's Guide to Action Research: Practical Connections for Implementation of Data-Driven Decision-Making by Mary E. Little, Dena D. Slanda, and Elizabeth Cramer

For a full list of books in this series, visit https://rowman.com/Action/SERIES/_/RLSELPP/Special-Education-Law,-Policy,-and-Practice.

The Educator's Guide to Action Research

Practical Connections for Implementation of Data-Driven Decision-Making

Mary E. Little
Dena D. Slanda
Elizabeth D. Cramer

ROWMAN & LITTLEFIELD
Lanham • Boulder • New York • London

Published by Rowman & Littlefield
An imprint of The Rowman & Littlefield Publishing Group, Inc.
4501 Forbes Boulevard, Suite 200, Lanham, Maryland 20706
www.rowman.com

86-90 Paul Street, London EC2A 4NE

Copyright © 2025 by The Rowman & Littlefield Publishing Group, Inc.

All rights reserved. No part of this book may be reproduced in any form or by any electronic or mechanical means, including information storage and retrieval systems, without written permission from the publisher, except by a reviewer who may quote passages in a review.

British Library Cataloguing in Publication Information Available

Library of Congress Cataloging-in-Publication Data

Names: Little, Mary E. (Professor of education), author. | Slanda, Dena, 1977– author. | Cramer, Elizabeth D., 1976– author.
Title: The educator's guide to action research : practical connections for implementation of data-driven decision-making / Mary E. Little, Dena D. Slanda, Elizabeth D. Cramer.
Description: Lanham, Maryland : Rowman & Littlefield, [2025] | Series: Special education law, policy, and practice | Includes bibliographical references and index.
Identifiers: LCCN 2024005888 (print) | LCCN 2024005889 (ebook) | ISBN 9781538177433 (cloth) | ISBN 9781538177440 (paperback) | ISBN 9781538177457 (ebook)
Subjects: LCSH: Action research in education. | Multi-tiered systems of support (Education) | School management and organization—Decision making—Data processing.
Classification: LCC LB1028.24 .L586 2025 (print) | LCC LB1028.24 (ebook) | DDC 370.72—dc23/eng/20240528
LC record available at https://lccn.loc.gov/2024005888
LC ebook record available at https://lccn.loc.gov/2024005889

Contents

Introduction   vii

1   Practical Application of Action Research   1
2   Equity-Based Action Research   17
3   Data Collection and Analysis   33
4   Multi-Tiered System of Supports   57
5   Data-Driven Decision-Making   73
6   Action Research Using Data-Driven Decision-Making within MTSS   97
7   Opportunities to Use and Share Action Research within Educational Settings   119

Index   135

Introduction

This book is designed to build and enhance the knowledge of teachers, teacher leaders, school-based educators, and families about the action research (AR) process, including the use of multiple sources of assessment data to inform instruction, interventions, services, and supports. Improved learning outcomes for all students are the responsibility of all school personnel as multiple school-based teams (for example, data, grade level, special education eligibility, multitiered system of support) facilitate the data-driven decision-making (DDDM) process with various sources and types of data. The team members may include students, parents, general educators, special educators, instructional coaches, administrators, and related service personnel (for example, school psychologists, speech-language pathologists, gifted specialists, occupational therapists, counselors). This resource will demystify the AR process and connect with other school-based DDDM processes, including decision-making during the implementation of the multi-tiered system of supports (MTSS). Descriptions of the phases, components, necessary skills, and examples of DDDM are explained and connected to other solution-finding opportunities as each contributes to a comprehensive system within our classrooms and schools. In addition, equity-focused approaches are described and infused within each of the topical contents to provide specific examples to ensure instruction, interventions, and assessments to address the diverse needs of all learners. Features of each chapter include chapter objectives, key terms, vignettes, reflective questions, resources, graphics, and summary questions to extend, enhance, and apply the learning.

RATIONALE

According to the US Department of Education (USDOE, 2022), the number of students aged five to twenty-one receiving special education services under the Individuals with Disabilities Act (IDEA), Part B continues to gradually rise each year, with 13.7 percent of students ages five to twenty-one receiving special education services. This phenomenon suggests students are potentially not receiving much-needed interventions prior to the determination of eligibility for services. These percentages are expected to continue to rise given the impact of the COVID-19 pandemic. It is predicted that student performance due to the missed instruction and interrupted learning caused by the COVID-19 pandemic has the potential to be misinterpreted as students with disabilities, which could lead to inappropriate referrals to special education (Van Dorn et al., 2020).

Simultaneously, US schools are becoming increasingly racially, ethnically, and linguistically diverse (RELD), with White, non-Hispanic students currently comprising less than half (45 percent) of the public school population (Irwin et al., 2023). The percentage of students with disabilities from RELD backgrounds is higher than their representation in the total public school population; this representation is increasing each year. Currently, 14 percent of US students receiving special education services are White and non-Hispanic (Harkins Monaco et al., 2023). Students from RELD backgrounds often face additional challenges in learning and demonstrating what they have learned. Many researchers believe these additional challenges are a product of unequally structured learning opportunities (for example, Avant, 2016), including lower teacher expectations, cultural differences in students' and teachers' behavioral expectations, language differences, and poverty (Harry and Klingner, 2022). This long history of educational inequities has led to challenges in academic, psychosocial, and behavioral outcomes for RELD students with or at risk for disabilities (Office of Special Education Programs, 2021). Therefore equitable prevention, intervention, and services for students with and without disabilities within classrooms and schools are even more critical. Further, students with and without disabilities may experience significant academic, behavioral, and social characteristics that require intensive, individualized interventions designed to address their persistent learning needs through individualization. Concomitantly, the majority of students across all disability categories (64.8 percent) is educated in the general education classroom for more than 80 percent of the school day (USDOE, 2022). Given the substantial number of students who require prevention, intervention, and specialized instruction and interventions in classrooms, all teachers, administrators, and family members need the necessary knowledge, skills, and resources to collaboratively develop, evaluate, and implement targeted instruction and interventions to improve all students' academic, behavior, and social emotional outcomes.

In addition, to address increasingly complex needs of diverse students and their families, interdisciplinary approaches are needed. Interdisciplinary approaches utilize equity-focused, culturally relevant engagement methods within the communities they serve to address the academic, behavioral, social emotional, and mental health needs of children and their families. These approaches engage multiple stakeholders: educators, families, caregivers, community members, and others. To achieve such coordinated support for children and their families in high-need communities, advanced interdisciplinary approaches and evidence-based practices across education departments, including school psychology and counseling, are needed to address the whole child. These innovative approaches to support students and their families in high-need communities result from the knowledge and implementation among educators with diverse knowledge and skills to leverage existing strengths across academic, social, behavioral, and emotional domains to support the growing needs of an increasingly diverse society through the use of MTSS (Every Student Succeeds Act, 2015). The overarching focus is to ensure that each child meets challenging academic standards, especially those at risk of educational failure or in need of special assistance and support, such as students who are living in poverty, who attend high-minority schools, and who have disabilities (USDOE, 2022).

BOUNDARY SPANNERS: CONNECTIONS ACROSS DISCIPLINES

Students in our schools are often not taught by well-prepared, highly qualified teachers due to decades of chronic teacher shortages. This issue has the highest impact on students of color and students in schools serving higher populations of low-income families. Teachers who receive thorough preparation and who are supported with high-quality professional learning opportunities throughout their careers are better equipped to meet the needs of all their students. In addition, well-prepared and supported teachers remain in the profession at higher rates than underprepared teachers. Effective preparation ensures that teachers are equipped to provide the powerful, deeper learning experiences that enable students to not only learn content but also think critically, solve problems, and learn how to learn (Patrick et al., 2023).

To address critical issues of student learning, innovative solutions through collaboration among educators from diverse disciplines (for example, general education teachers, special education teachers, school psychologists, interventionists) are needed to connect theoretical knowledge and diverse expertise into job-embedded practices. High-quality and sustained professional learning is a critical building block to address the diverse learning needs of students. This requires a collaborative, connected, and sustained model of professional learning that envisions and develops shared understandings, knowledge, and practices to coconstruct reconceptualized roles, opportunities, and responsibilities for faculty, service providers, administrators, and family members. This requires educators and family members to partner and engage in collaborative, critical conversations to address previously held beliefs, practices, and procedures innovatively. The purpose of this book is to challenge current beliefs, knowledge, and practices in action research, solution-finding, and DDDM within the MTSS framework to comprehensively engage in collaborative professional learning and implementation of practical, classroom and school-based practices to enhance the learning for all students.

SPECIFIC CONNECTIONS

The rationale for the enhanced and systematic use of DDDM within an MTSS framework is to integrate and focus instruction and interventions to the specific, data-driven needs of each individual student. Common knowledge, language, and practices of collaborative DDDM within a school-wide MTSS framework can serve to (a) provide a process to identify and use instructional and intensive interventions; (b) facilitate increased implementation of evidence-based instructional methods, strategies, and resources; (c) monitor and document student learning through continuous progress monitoring; and (d) increase the speed and efficiency of service identification and delivery that improve student performance. Educators, service providers, administrators, and family members need information on the process of DDDM, definitions and examples of evidence-based instruction, researched interventions, and definitions and examples of classroom assessments to continuously monitor student progress to realize the benefits for improved student achievement for all students.

Within the past few years, the use of classroom DDDM (also referred to as action research, critical inquiry, and problem solving) as a means for school improvement and professional development has increased. For the purposes of this book, the term "data-driven decision-making" will be the term used to describe the decision-making process used by teachers and others to solve instructional (academic and behavioral) issues, concerns, and problems within their classrooms and schools. This process can be used for several reasons:

- to continuously monitor student learning for adjustments to teaching, methods, resources, etc.;
- to collect student learning for accountability purposes from school, district, and/or state mandates;
- to aggregate and summarize achievement data for additional professional purposes;
- to include as part of a continuous process of decision-making at the program level through school-wide initiatives related to intervention teams, special education processes, and/or MTSS; and
- to complete classroom research related to specific classroom instructional techniques or processes (action research).

Action research is defined as a process in which teachers systematically reflect on their practice and make changes to their instruction based on careful analysis of current classroom performance information of their students. Unlike traditional research, in which researchers study the teachers, action research is conducted by classroom teachers in an effort to improve student learning in their classrooms. During action research, the teacher becomes the primary researcher. As researchers, teachers are key to analyzing instructional concerns and individual student issues within their classrooms. After collecting information related to the problem identified, the teacher, in collaboration with others, makes decisions about the content, methods, and/or strategies to resolve the identified instructional concern. Through continuously monitoring the results of the decisions, teachers then determine the effectiveness of the decisions made related to the desired goals for the students. This interactive, cyclical, and dynamic process approach to instructional DDDM involves knowledge of data collection, evidence-based instructional practices and resources, and informal and diagnostic assessments to continuously monitor student results by teachers and other educators within classrooms. This process is integral and utilized within the MTSS framework to continuously address issues and develop solutions to student learning.

Coordination and continued communication among each of the educational partners provide valuable input for continuous improvement within a system of school reform based on student results (Gesel et al., 2021) through the expert use of DDDM on MTSS teams. The coordination of service delivery continues to provide more intensive instruction and interventions to identified students through DDDM by teams of teachers and school-based educators on various school teams that use DDDM. Descriptions, examples, and resources related to the implementation of DDDM by individual teachers and other professionals to address the academic and behavioral needs of groups of students and individual students within the MTSS framework are included in subsequent chapters of this book. In addition, another chapter of this book focuses on equity-based approaches within the AR process that includes the use of culturally sustaining assessments, evidence-based strategies, and interventions to meet the needs of *all* students, including those from RELD backgrounds and other minoritized students.

ABOUT THIS BOOK

The Educator's Guide to Action Research: Practical Connections for Implementation of Data-Driven Decision-Making is an interactive, practical resource for teachers, other educators, and family members to actively participate in the DDDM process within the MTSS framework in classrooms and schools with the goal of improved student achievement for all students. Each chapter provides step-by-step approaches, resources, and examples to develop common understandings, language, and processes to conduct DDDM including descriptions of each phase, reflective activities, planning forms, and concrete, real-life examples. This DDDM process will be described within the context of the MTSS framework. Due to the applied focus, the examples, planning forms, charts, and case studies included in this book will be applicable to all educators interested in using data for classroom instructional DDDM. Action research is a cyclical and continuous process. However, for the purpose of describing and modeling the process in these resources, the tiers of the MTSS framework and phases of DDDM and action research will be described in a linear fashion.

NEXT STEPS WITH YOUR LEARNING AND USING DDDM

Comprehensive DDDM processes utilize the knowledge, skills, and phases of action research within classrooms and schools by all educators, including special and general education teachers, school psychologists, and other related service personnel, within one system of data use for instruction, interventions, and determination of needed services and supports within the MTSS framework. This book will address content by extending educators' knowledge and skills to collect, analyze, and utilize data to effectively plan, teach, assess, and provide interventions for students within comprehensive systems of data use and decision-making. This user-friendly book will serve as both a reference and a practical resource guide. Each chapter connects research to practice and extends learning through case studies, vignettes, samples, practical strategies, real-world context, links to resources, and end-of-chapter discussion questions. The content in each of the subsequent chapters in this book focuses on specific knowledge and skills within the following topics.

Chapter 1: Practical Application of Action Research

This chapter sets the framework for action research by providing definitions; sharing common language; describing history, benefits, and approaches to action research; and connecting DDDM within the AR process. In addition, practical considerations and necessary professional learning to implement DDDM within the AR processes are shared.

Chapter 2: Equity-Based Action Research

The content of this chapter focuses on equity as the foundation of DDDM, including the AR process. This chapter emphasizes the critical need for educators to be culturally competent and culturally relevant in their approaches to DDDM and action research in their classrooms and schools. A large focus of this equity-based approach includes the use of culturally sustaining assessments, evidence-based strategies, and interventions to meet the needs of *all* students, including those from culturally and linguistically diverse (CLD) backgrounds and other minoritized students. Action research is described in culturally responsive and equitable ways, including engaging parents and family members in the process. Topics include information about culturally relevant and sustaining teaching approaches, equitable approaches to DDDM, and action research including appropriate action research approaches, assessment considerations, and building collaborative partnerships.

Chapter 3: Data Collection and Analysis

This chapter focuses on types of assessments, data collection, and analysis. Rationale and descriptions of various assessments, including teacher-made tests, standardized assessments, and observational data, are described for data collection in academic and behavioral settings. Also, practical guidelines and examples are provided for identifying, constructing, using, and understanding data collection assessments. Several templates for data collection, analyses, and reflection are provided.

Chapter 4: Multi-Tiered System of Supports

MTSS is a framework for providing students with high-quality, evidence-based instruction and intervention that is responsive to their strengths and needs. This chapter (a) details the essential components of the MTSS framework, including the tiers of instruction and intervention, DDDM, and evidence-based practice; (b) discusses how the framework is designed to support students in academics, behavior, and social-emotional development; and (c) introduces how action research fits within an MTSS framework.

Chapter 5: Data-Driven Decision-Making

This chapter calls for teachers, instructional coaches, and other classroom and school-based educators to consider why DDDM and action research within classrooms and schools are integral to meeting the instructional, behavioral, and social emotional needs of students with diverse learning needs. Consistent with federal legislation (for example, Every Student Succeeds Act, 2015), educators work within an MTSS framework for data collection, analysis, and intervention. This chapter provides educators with descriptions, templates, resources, and tools necessary to complete the phases of DDDM within the MTSS framework.

Chapter 6: Action Research Using Data-Driven Decision-Making within MTSS

Each phase in the DDDM process is discussed in detail with a focus on educators' roles, responsibilities, and tasks throughout the phases within the AR cycle that is implemented within each tier of the MTSS framework. The four phases of the DDDM process are revisited and described in detail as related to examples. Considerations for classroom implementation of instructional plans are then discussed related to fidelity and determining a data collection plan for progress monitoring. This continuous cycle is integral to successful instruction and interventions within MTSS processes and student learning within the classroom and school. This chapter provides educators with descriptions and opportunities to apply knowledge, resources, and tools necessary to complete DDDM within the MTSS framework with two case studies.

Chapter 7: Opportunities to Use and Share Action Research within Educational Settings

This chapter focuses on the use and sharing of the AR findings, ranging from the personal level as an educator through wider dissemination practices, including with school teams, key stakeholders, and the professional educational community. Descriptions of the most common and practical approaches for organizing and sharing different types of data are provided for different purposes and audiences. In addition, discussions and examples for sharing the results with parents, other school-based educators, and/or publications and presentations will be described. The connections to the sharing of research-based findings to being an educational leader are explored.

REFERENCES

Avant, D. W. (2016). Using response to intervention/multi-tiered systems of supports to promote social justice in schools. *Journal for Multicultural Education, 10*(4), 507–20. https://doi.org/10.1108/jme-06-2015-0019

Every Student Succeeds Act of 2015, Pub. L. No. 114-95 114 § Stat. 117 (2015). https://congress.gov/114/plaws/publ95/PLAW-114publ95.pdf

Gesel, S. A., LeJeune, L. M., Chow, J. C., Sinclair, A. C., and Lemons, C. J. (2021). A meta-analysis of the impact of professional development on teachers' knowledge, skill, and self-efficacy in data-based decision-making. *Journal of Learning Disabilities, 54*(4), 269–83.

Harkins Monaco, E. A., Brusnahan, L. S., and Fuller, M. (2023). Guidance for the antiracist educator: Culturally sustaining pedagogies for disability and diversity. *Teaching Exceptional Children, 55*(5), 296–99. https://doi.org/10.1177/00400599211046281

Harry, B., and Klingner, J. (2022). *Why are so many students of color in special education?: Understanding race and disability in schools.* Teachers College Press.

Irwin, V., Wang, K., Tezil, T., Zhang, J., Filbey, A., Jung, J., Bullock Mann, F., Dilig, R., and Parker, S. (2023). Report on the condition of education 2023 (NCES 2023-144rev). US Department of Education. Washington, DC: National Center for Education Statistics. Retrieved September 7, 2023, from https://nces.ed.gov/pubsearch/pubsinfo.asp?pubid=2023144rev.

Office of Special Education Programs. (2021). Individuals with Disabilities Education Act (IDEA) database. US Department of Education. https://www2.ed.gov/programs/osepidea/618-data/state-level-datafiles/index.html#bcc

Patrick, S. K., Darling-Hammond, L., and Kini, T. (2023). Educating teachers in California: What matters for teacher preparedness? Learning Policy Institute. https://doi.org/10.54300/956.678

US Department of Education (USDOE). (2022). 43rd annual report to Congress on the implementation of the Individuals with Disabilities Education Act 2021. Office of Special Education and Rehabilitative Services.

Van Dorn, A., Cooney, R. E., and Sabin, M. L. (2020). COVID-19 exacerbating inequalities in the US. *The Lancet, 395*(10232), 1243–44.

Chapter One

Practical Application of Action Research

INTRODUCTION

This chapter sets the framework for action research by providing definitions; sharing common language; describing history, benefits, and approaches to action research; and connecting data-driven decision-making (DDDM) within the action research (AR) process. In addition, practical considerations and necessary professional learning to implement DDDM within the AR processes are shared.

OBJECTIVES

After reading this chapter, the reader will be able to

- learn about and compare the DDDM process of action research with traditional research,
- describe the components of the DDDM process, and
- discuss the benefits and types of action research using the DDDM process.

KEY TERMS

Action research: To study an authentic classroom and/or school situation with the view to improve the quality of actions and results with the use of multiple sources of data.
Data-driven decision-making (DDDM): The effective use of data by teachers and educators with developed knowledge and skills to analyze data to improve instruction.
Data-based individualization (DBI): The systematic use of assessment data to monitor student progress and provide intensified interventions. DBI allows teachers to determine if an intervention is improving student outcomes with concrete information to adjust instruction.

Evidence-based practices: Instructional or behavior practices that are research based and when implemented with fidelity have been shown to have a statistically significant impact on student achievement (Cook and Odom, 2013).

Fidelity of implementation: The degree to which an intervention or program is delivered as developed and intended.

Multi-tiered system of supports (MTSS): According the Every Student Succeeds Act, MTSS is a "comprehensive continuum of evidence-based, systemic practices to support rapid response to students' needs, with regular observation to facilitate data-based instructional decision making" (Every Student Succeeds Act, 2015, Section 8002(10)(33)).

Qualitative research: Methods of traditional research that use narrative, descriptive approaches to data collection to understand identified educational questions and/or issues to inform actions and meaning from the perspectives of research participants.

Quantitative research: Methods of traditional research that focus on controlling variables to determine cause/effect relationships and/or the strength of those relationships.

Traditional research: multiple methods to explain, predict, and/or control educational issues.

VIGNETTE

I finished a whole group instruction lesson with my first graders, and they were now working independently for more practice. Some of my students worked diligently, while others seemed uninterested or disengaged. A few weren't "getting it" as quickly as I had hoped. Seeing them appear confused and unmotivated after my lesson made me think about the AR workshop I attended yesterday. There was a lot of information presented in the workshop. The presenter talked about the use of assessment data to make decisions about instruction, differentiation, interventions, and progress monitoring to meet our students' needs. Although I brought back a lot of good information to share with my colleagues, I wish I had asked more questions during the workshop for clarification. I know I must find a way to teach all my students, particularly those who struggle with the content and specific skills, but I am a little overwhelmed by the AR process of using assessment data to make instructional decisions in my classroom. I already feel that there is so much to know and do with testing my students, the pressures of paperwork, new curriculum mandates by my district, etc. Perhaps I am fearful about DDDM within the AR process. What is it, and how does it work? Where and how do I begin this process? How can and will it work for me and my students? But most of all, what is my role in this process? I want all my students to be successful. I know I want to change whatever I am doing to help my students.

—Ms. Hernandez, first-grade teacher

DECISION-MAKING IN CLASSROOMS

As educators, we know that high-quality instruction by caring and knowledgeable teachers matters. According to almost four decades of research (Hattie, 2012), students can learn when provided with effective teaching with evidence-based practices. In our classrooms and schools, multiple federal and state requirements have increased the emphasis on accountability for improved achievement in rigorous content for all students through effective teaching. While schools must work within federal, state, and local regulations and policies, teachers, coaches, and instructional staff have significant autonomy every school day to determine the scope and sequence of their daily lesson plans, instructional practices, assessment decisions, and classroom procedures. Without question, student success is determined by the knowledge and skills of teachers and school-based educators. However, educators must also adhere to and implement required regulations, policies, and procedures while meeting the academic and behavioral needs of their students. How do educators like Ms. Hernandez improve student learning for each of the students in her classroom?

DDDM within an AR process provides a continuous improvement model for teachers and other educators to integrate and focus instruction and interventions to the specific needs of students. DDDM can serve to (a) provide a process to identify and use various instructional practices and interventions; (b) facilitate increased implementation of effective, evidence-based practices, strategies, and resources; (c) monitor and document student progress through continuous progress monitoring, and (d) increase the speed, determination, and efficiency of potential, additional educational services needed by individual students to improve student learning.

Within the past few years, DDDM has also been used as a means for school improvement and professional development, as well as a process to describe the impact of professional development related to student learning (Muñoz and Guskey, 2015). For the purposes of this book, the term "data-driven decision-making" is the term used to describe the decision-making process used by teachers and other educators to solve instructional (academic and behavioral) issues, concerns, and problems within classrooms and schools. This process is used by teachers and other educators (for example, instructional coaches, curriculum leaders, school psychologists, interventionists) for several reasons:

- to continuously monitor student learning for adjustments to teaching, methods, resources, etc.;
- to collect evidence of student learning for accountability purposes from school, district, and/or state mandates;
- to identify, review, and summarize achievement data for additional professional purposes (for example, professional portfolios, university courses, etc.);
- to include as part of a continuous process of decision-making at the classroom level through school-wide initiatives related to intervention teams, special education processes, and/or implementation of MTSS; and
- to complete classroom action research related to specific classroom instructional techniques or processes.

The goal for making decisions for each of these purposes is to improve student learning through data collection, analyses, and interpretation using a systematic, continuous improvement framework. Whether collecting data as traditional educational research, action research, or problem solving within school teams (for example, grade level, MTSS, eligibility for specific educational services), there are four steps within a DDDM framework:

1. Identify: Use data to identify classroom or school-based area of need.
2. Develop and Implement: In response to the data, develop and implement an intervention plan using evidence-based practices.
3. Collect and Analyze: After sufficient time, collect assessment data to determine results from the intervention.
4. Reflect and Share: After analyzing the data, reflect and share results, taking actions as decided (see figure 1.1).

TYPES OF RESEARCH

Each of these four steps within DDDM will be described in much detail in subsequent chapters in this book. Although these four steps are integral, core steps within DDDM, the approaches, methods, and procedures are different depending on the goals. The goal for traditional research in education is to explain, predict, and/or control educational issues. Once a specific research question(s) is identified after a thorough review of published findings and other sources of available assessment data and information, traditional research has multiple methods to investigate specific interventions or describe results. The area of focus or research question identified by the researcher will determine the most appropriate approach (quantitative and/or qualitative) to use.

Quantitative research focuses on controlling variables to determine cause/effect relationships and/or the strength of those relationships. This type of research uses numbers to quantify the cause/effect relationship. For example, researchers may be interested in studying the effects of a certain reading program (independent variable) on the rate at which students learn to read (dependent variable) to address the identified need of improving student reading levels. The researchers may hypothesize that the identified reading program (intervention) will shorten the time needed to learn to read by the students. To confirm or reject this hypothesis, a detailed implementation plan for the intervention is delivered to one group of students (experimental), while a similar group of students is taught without the identified reading program (control group or business as usual). Students are randomly assigned to either of the groups. At the end of the implementation timeline (experiment), assessment data are collected and analyzed from both groups of students to determine whether the hypothesis could be accepted or rejected with a predetermined level of statistical significance. Finally, researchers reflect and summarize the process and results from the educational research and share the results either through a thesis, dissertation, presentation, or publication. (See Hoy, 2016, or Johnson and Christensen, 2016, for examples of books on quantitative research.)

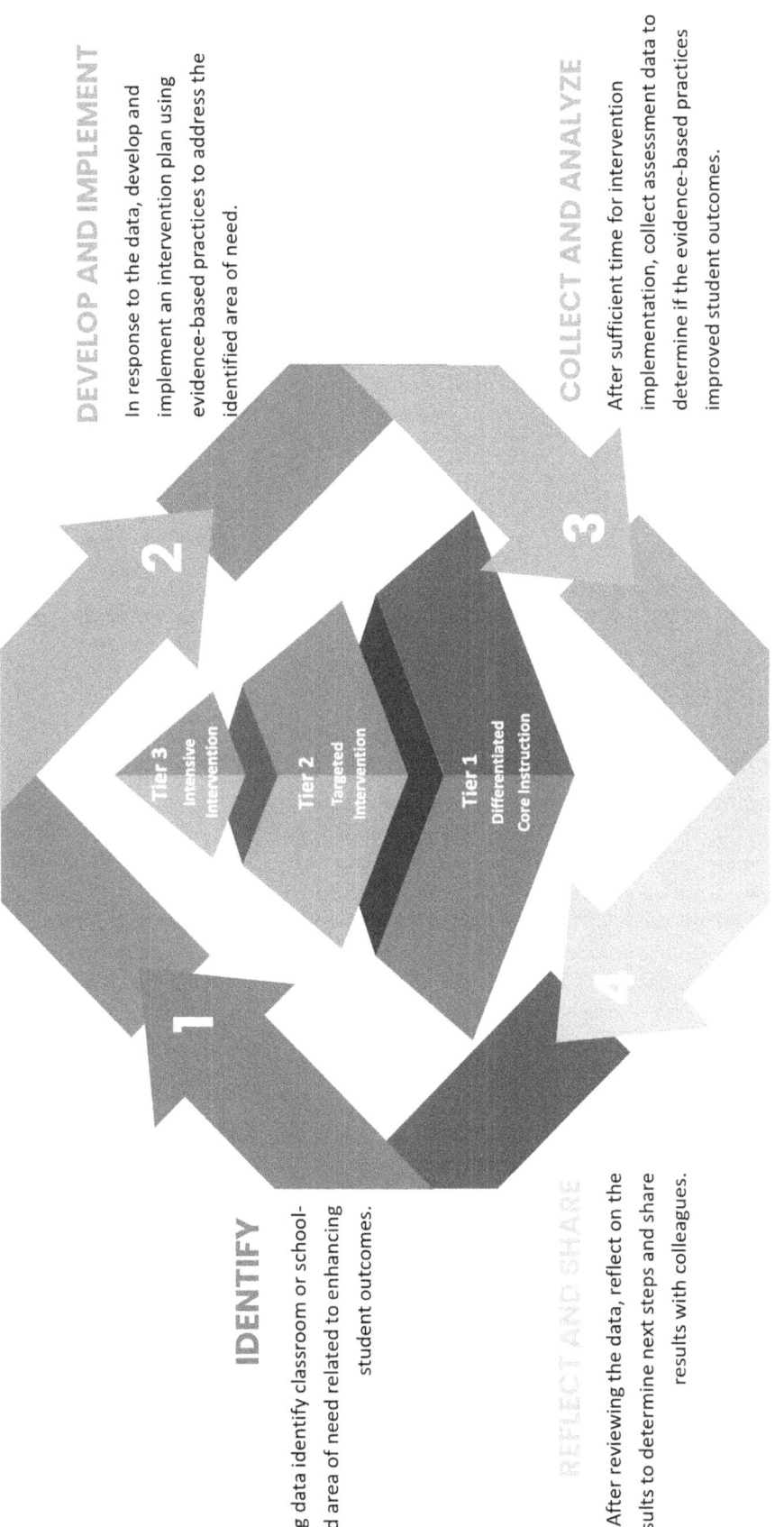

Figure 1.1. Data-Driven Decision-Making Process.

Table 1.1. Comparison of Traditional and Action Research across Components

DDDM Components	Traditional Research	Action Research
Identify	Review of research identifies research question/topic. Conducted through formalized research courses with university mentors.	Conducted by school-based educators to address needs identified through school-based assessment data of identified issues.
Develop; Implement	Based on research question(s), specific designs, methods, and procedures are developed and implemented as approved by external research committee.	School-based researchers choose an area of focus, determine data collection techniques, and implement evidence-based instruction/interventions.
Collect; Analyze	Data collected as per research design are analyzed as per accepted methods and procedures and reviewed by committee members.	Data are collected from identified classroom and school-based assessments and analyzed by members of school-based data teams.
Reflect; Share	Researcher reflects and summarizes the process and results and shares the results either through a thesis, dissertation, presentation, or publication, as accepted by committee members/external reviewers.	Educational teams review shared data to determine what actions need to be taken to refine, improve, or maintain learning within the classroom or with additional interventions and/or supports.

Qualitative research in education uses narrative, descriptive approaches to data collection to understand identified educational questions and/or issues to inform actions and meaning from the perspectives of research participants. Research questions are again identified after a thorough review of the educational issue. Qualitative approaches might include, for example, observations, interviews, reviews of student products, and other sources of information to understand, reflect, and share results. For example, researchers may want to understand teachers' perceptions about a reading program. The researcher may observe in classrooms, interview teachers implementing the program, interview students receiving this instruction, and review various instructional and intervention components of the program to identify themes about the reading program. These results could also then be shared and disseminated as a thesis, dissertation, presentation, or publication. (See Anfara and Mertz, 2015, or Creswell, 2013, for examples of books on qualitative research.)

Action research is defined as a process in which teachers systematically reflect on their practice and make changes to their instruction based on careful analysis of current assessment data of their students. Unlike traditional research in which researchers study the teachers, action research is conducted by classroom teachers with the goal of improving student learning within their classrooms. During action research, the teacher becomes the primary researcher. As researchers, teachers are key to analyzing instructional concerns and individual student issues within their classrooms. After collecting information related to the problem identified, the teacher makes decisions about the best resources, methods, and/or strategies to resolve the identified instructional concern. Through continuously monitoring the results of the decisions, teachers then determine the effectiveness of the decisions related to the desired goals for the students. This interactive and dynamic DDDM process involves knowledge of data collection, evidence-based instructional practices and resources, and informal and curriculum-based assessments to continuously monitor student learning. For purposeful changes in the teaching and learning process to occur, teachers and students must be involved in the decisions that directly affect the process. As educators engage in the AR process, they become agents of change. The foundation of action research asserts that educational problems and issues are best identified and investigated at the classroom and school levels. By integrating action research into classrooms and schools, findings can be applied immediately and problems solved more quickly (Muñoz and Guskey, 2015).

Therefore traditional research and action research utilize the four steps of DDDM as described (figure 1.1) but follow additional, specific procedures, methods, and resources depending on the educational goal to investigate. Table 1.1 provides an overview of the types of research related to the four steps of the DDDM framework. Throughout this book, connections, descriptions, and examples of the four-step process of DDDM are focused, described, and clarified as related to the process of action research by teachers and school-based educators. In addition, DDDM is described, connected, and illuminated with specific examples within the context of differentiation of instruction in classrooms, determination and use of interventions, and continuous informal assessments to improve learning and results for our students with diverse needs within the framework of MTSS.

Stop and Reflect:

How would you describe the differences between traditional research and action research to other teachers at your school? How is action research related to other responsibilities of teachers and other educators in schools?

ORIGINS AND MODELS OF ACTION RESEARCH

Action research is a process where educators study student learning related to their own teaching. The term "action research" was described by Kurt Lewin (1952) to give "credence to the development of powers of reflective thought, discussion, decision, and action by ordinary people participating in research to address 'private troubles' that they have in common" (Adelman, 1993, p. 8). Subsequent theorists and researchers (for example, Dewey, Elliott) followed and enhanced this focus on reflective thought and action to address instructional and social issues identified at the classroom and school site (Elliott, 1991). Conducting action research provides educators with a process to reflect on one's own teaching practices and engage in self-directed learning with the ultimate goal of improving student learning. For students to reach optimal learning, educators must continuously build upon their knowledge of student learning and intentionally study the instructional practices and interventions they are implementing in the classroom. Action research is planned inquiry—a deliberate search for truth, information, or knowledge (Schmuck, 1997). For teachers, specific questions to reflect on include the following:

Do you purposefully observe and assess your students to determine areas of change?
Do you design instructional plans to actualize the change?
Do you continuously monitor your instruction to ensure that the change has occurred to improve student learning?

These are reflective questions of critical inquiry that teachers use during the AR process. When educators conduct action research, they are deliberate about the data they collect, the decisions they make, and the lessons they teach. "Action research is a natural extension of good teaching. Observing students closely, analyzing their needs, and adjusting the curriculum to fit the needs of all students have always been important skills demonstrated by fine teachers" (Hubbard and Power, 1999, p. 1). When teachers conduct action research, they ask themselves a critical question: "Am I making an impact on student learning?" When teachers notice a lack of learning by students, they systematically and intentionally plan instruction and/or interventions to meet the needs of their students. The primary goal of action research is to improve student learning by developing and refining the skills of teaching. This is empowering for teachers, giving them opportunities to grow within their professional roles and responsibilities.

> Stop and Reflect:
>
> Consider Ms. Hernandez and her concerns as described in the vignette. She appeared to notice a lack of engagement and learning by some of the students in her class. What specifically was she observing? What additional information could she review to determine the students' needs? What could be some next steps to develop and implement a plan to engage students in the lesson?

Action research is a continuous and reflective process in which educators make instructional decisions in their classrooms based on student needs, as reflected by classroom data. As mentioned earlier, there are four phases within this DDDM process within all types of research. Action research never really ends because learning is a cyclical process. An action researcher continuously observes, analyzes designs, assesses, and adjusts. The cyclical nature of action research provides teachers with ongoing opportunities to reflect on and refine their own teaching practices. Figure 1.1 displays the continuous nature of the process. This process may sound straightforward. However, it is difficult to control all the factors that affect outcomes and results in classrooms and schools. Consider for a moment the factors that affect learning outcomes within classrooms. Are the necessary materials available? Are the students engaged in the lesson? Does the teacher have the expertise for this lesson? Action researchers acknowledge and embrace these complications rather than try to control them. So why learn about and use DDDM of action research within our classrooms and schools? What are the benefits and opportunities for using this DDDM process? What are some of the concerns? How does this process connect with other assessment processes for data analyses and use within other frameworks and processes in my school? The next section describes benefits, characteristics, and considerations of action research.

BENEFITS OF ACTION RESEARCH

Action research provides many benefits to students, teachers, and schools. Students benefit because their learning is the focus. Instructional practices are being designed to accelerate learning and build upon student knowledge. Close monitoring is occurring throughout the process to ensure that appropriate progress is being made and, if not, adjustments in instruction will occur. Teachers benefit because the process allows them to reflect on, study, and refine their own professional practice. By participating in action research, the teacher develops a sense of ownership in the knowledge constructed, and this sense of ownership heavily contributes to the possibilities for real change to take place in the classroom (Mertler, 2020). Conducting action research that focuses on implementing new instructional practices can bridge professional development into actual practice, as there is often a lack of connection between more traditional research and classroom practices. Many teachers who participate in action research find it very empowering because they have actual evidence that they have made an impact on their students' learning. Teachers who engage in action research depend on themselves as decision makers and gain more confidence in their decisions about curriculum and instruction (Green et al., 2016). The AR process encourages collaboration among diverse educators. Schools benefit because student achievement can improve when student learning is being studied, and specific learning needs are being addressed through continuous focus on instruction and intervention based on data. When teachers are engaged in collaborative action research, and the process is well supported, a professional learning community encourages professional dialogue, learning, and research with a focus on student learning. Additionally, this process can assist school personnel in gathering data to evaluate the effectiveness of their instructional practices and professional development that can be useful and beneficial in numerous settings, team meetings, and professional learning communities.

> Stop and Reflect:
>
> Take a moment and reflect on why you should conduct DDDM within action research. What are the benefits of action research to teachers and students? How could participating in this AR process impact your teaching? What are some current opportunities within your school? Do you have concerns about conducting action research in your classroom?

APPROACHES TO ACTION RESEARCH

Action research is a process that teachers can use in their classrooms to address instructional questions and challenges. Within this process, teachers and other school personnel may choose to focus on one student, a small group of students, a class or several classes, or an entire school. Three approaches to action research have been described: individual teacher action research, collaborative action research, and school-wide action research. Even though the settings and collaborators are different, the process of DDDM within action research remains the same. (Refer back to figure 1.1.)

Individual teacher action research focuses on studying a problem or concern within a single classroom. The teacher who engages in individual teacher research may or may not have support from colleagues and administration to share, brainstorm, and discuss the focus of action research. Although one teacher may implement action research, support from knowledgeable educators within the school or district is still important for successful individual teacher action research to occur. Also, universities, educational agencies, and districts may encourage teacher action research by providing ongoing professional learning related to the needs of the individual teacher-researcher. These opportunities may also provide different methods for teachers to share the results of their action research.

Collaborative action research focuses on studying a problem or concern within one or more classrooms. Teachers may collaborate and work together to study a particular classroom concern in many ways. Several examples of collaborative action research include

- coteachers in one classroom studying a specific group of students,
- a team of teachers focusing on student learning when implementing a new curriculum product and/or evidence-based practice, and
- a group of teachers in the same school investigating instruction to address new curriculum standards.

This collaborative AR approach fosters a joint effort because more than one teacher is involved in a specific area of study. Opportunities for sharing and dialogue are more likely to occur, especially within established teams in schools.

School-wide action research occurs when faculty members are involved in studying a specific concern identified from school-wide data. This approach requires a great deal of support from the administrators and lead teachers/personnel, but the results can lead to school-wide change. Successful school-wide action research is directly related to initiatives contained within the school improvement plan. An environment that is most supportive of the school-wide AR process provides the following:

- teams of teachers and/or other educators (for example, grade-level teams, data teams, professional learning communities),
- a school or environment that fosters teacher learning, including professional development and coaching (for example, instructional coach or peer coach),
- planned time to reanalyze action research, and
- a supportive environment, including administration. (Calhoun, 1994)

Please refer to table 1.2 for examples of research questions that can be studied with action research using DDDM.

Table 1.2. Approaches to Action Research

Approaches	Level of Focus	Level of Participation	Example of Research Question
Individual	Single classroom	Individual teacher	1. What impact can daily phonemic awareness activities have on my kindergarten students' oral language development? (*Kindergarten teacher*) 2. How can using concrete objects (manipulatives) improve my students' ability to identify and extend patterns in mathematics? (*Third-grade teacher*)
Collaborative	One or more classrooms	Coteachers, teams, departments, educational agencies and teachers, university faculty and teachers, teachers within a district, etc.	1. How can students with disabilities experiencing deficits in phonemic awareness show improvement in those skills by participating in additional and intensive instruction in phonemic awareness activities at least four times per week? How will it affect their overall reading ability? (*Exceptional Student Education [ESE] teacher and literacy coach*) 2. How can implementing "Organizing Together," a Strategic Instruction Model curriculum, improve sixth graders' abilities to come to class organized and prepared? (*Sixth-grade teachers in a middle school team*)
School-wide	School improvement	Whole faculty	1. How can we teach our students to organize, analyze, synthesize, and interpret what they read? (*School-wide question*) 2. How can modeling through read-alouds improve students' abilities to organize, analyze, synthesize, and interpret what they read? 3. How can implementing a school-wide positive behavior support program improve students' safety and increase appropriate student behaviors within the school? (*All faculty*)

GETTING STARTED WITH DDDM AND ACTION RESEARCH

As noted earlier, the DDDM process of action research is not another new thing. Rather, this process addresses instructional questions by teachers and other school personnel by considering existing personnel, resources, and materials to address identified instructional concerns. It could be used in a more coherent and interrelated way to improve instruction for all students and to reduce the number of students struggling to learn within classrooms and schools. It is important to identify connections and uses of the DDDM process within the current professional opportunities in classrooms and schools. Each classroom, school, and district have different curricula, resources, personnel, and supports for teachers and students to ensure content mastery for all students. What opportunities are currently within your school to address the instructional needs of students struggling to learn? Consider what resources are available (for example, personnel, materials, time, and funds). How can these resources be leveraged and maximized to ensure that the necessary resources to meet students' academic and behavioral needs are identified and used? How do teachers differentiate core instruction within classrooms? What evidence-based interventions and intervention programs are available for students needing more targeted interventions? What personnel with specialized knowledge and skills (for example, instructional coach, special education teacher) are available to provide intensive interventions for individual students not mastering the content standard as demonstrated on classroom assessments? To address each student's instructional needs within classrooms and schools, a comprehensive system of instruction and interventions using various sources of data is implemented in numerous individual and team settings in our schools. Let's consider our school's resources, supports, and practices as we reflect on our opportunities for learning and use of DDDM within the AR processes (see table 1.3).

On a daily basis, educators strive to improve learning and outcomes for all students within classrooms, schools, and districts. This goal is achieved through the knowledge of and skillful use of assessment data, evidence-based practices, and interventions by teachers and other school professionals individually, with others, or within a school-wide system of continuous improvement. Availability and expert use of available assessments, practices, and instructional resources to address identified instructional needs are critical in this process. Screening measures, diagnostic assessments, and continuous progress monitoring of students' learning provide data and ongoing feedback to teachers to inform instruction. Beyond yielding targeted, differentiated instruction, DDDM can be enhanced, implemented, and monitored as part of mandated accountability, as well as considered before referrals for additional services, including special education for identified students, are made. In response to national trends and legislation such as the Every Student Succeeds Act (2015), educators are increasing the use of data to inform decisions that guide instruction and intervention for all learners within a MTSS framework. Within classrooms in our schools, MTSS promotes a coherent and intentional system of instruction by connecting multiple factors to enhance student learning. Ideally, MTSS provides and matches high-quality instructional practices and curricular resources to students' strengths and needs academically, socially, and behaviorally (Poortman and Schildkamp, 2016).

Table 1.3. Considerations When Implementing DDDM within Action Research

When initiating or expanding efforts of DDDM within the AR process in schools, complete the following table to identify needed resources and supports within your school.

Component	Findings	Next Steps
What are the sources of data? Are they accessible to teachers? Are they within a data management system that is available, accessible, and useful for instruction and intervention as aligned with state and district benchmarks?		
How do individual, collaborative, and school-wide data teams work?		
How is time allocated for professional development, collaboration, teaming, and additional intervention needed for identified students?		
What is done to strengthen core instruction across the school? How are these plans to be completed and supported?		
What types of evidence-based programs for instruction and interventions are available? What professional development is provided to learn about and use these resources with expertise and fidelity?		

Stop and Reflect:

Take a moment and reflect on the resources and procedures currently within your school to address the instructional needs of students struggling to learn. Consider what resources are available (for example, personnel, materials, time, and funds). How can these resources be leveraged and maximized to ensure that the necessary resources to meet students' academic and behavioral needs are identified and used by individual teachers and/or teams (for example, data teams, MTSS, etc.)?

> Stop and Reflect:
>
> In the vignette, Ms. Hernandez is observing some initial concerns for several of the students in her class. The use of multiple sources of data (for example, assessments, observations, reviews of student products, etc.) provides individuals and groups of teachers and other educators with information to identify an instructional concern, develop and implement an intervention plan, and collect and analyze results. Consider the students in your classroom and review various sources of data to identify an instructional concern. As you consider developing an intervention plan, complete table 1.3 to identify needed resources and supports within your school to implement your plan to address the identified area of need.

SUMMARY

DDDM within the AR process provides a continuous improvement model for teachers and other educators to integrate and focus instruction and interventions on specific, data-driven needs of students. The four-step process in DDDM includes: identify instructional needs of one or more students, develop and implement an intervention plan, collect and analyze data, and reflect and share the results. Although methods, resources, and procedures between traditional research and action research vary, the process and ultimate goal of DDDM focus on improved student achievement. Teachers and other educators can implement DDDM individually or with collaborative teams and focus on instructional concerns of one student, groups of students, or students throughout the school (Gesel et al., 2021). Considerations and supports when implementing DDDM and action research within schools are also similar. Specifically, guidelines for successful AR implementation within multiple school structures include the following:

- Establish diverse and multiple teams that use a DDDM process that includes teachers as well as other educators with varying expertise.
- Comprehensively map current initiatives, resources, and supports in place related to improving student achievement and supporting teachers and other educators in the areas of curriculum, instruction, and assessment.
- Communicate with and encourage participation by key stakeholders (for example, teachers, school psychologists, interventionists, administrators, and other service providers).
- Complete a comprehensive needs assessment and action plan for AR implementation, including vision, skills, incentives, and resources.
- Provide time for planning, professional development, meetings, and ongoing monitoring and evaluation.
- Complete comprehensive resource mapping and consider developing school-wide use of assessments, evidence-based instruction, and interventions that use current resources (for example, school-wide after-school tutoring programs).
- Develop and prepare an implementation manual detailing procedures, expectations, specific forms, and time frames for each tier and step of the MTSS process.

KEY TAKEAWAYS

DDDM has four key steps and multiple uses by individual teachers, data teams, and school personnel for traditional and action research.

The four key steps in the DDDM process include: identify, develop and implement, collect and analyze, and reflect and share (see figure 1.1).

The DDDM process within action research has multiple benefits and uses by teachers and other school-based educators to address the learning needs of students.

DDDM and action research are integral to implementation of MTSS within schools.

Resources and supports to assure quality implementation are necessary.

Where can I find information about action research and DDDM?

Resource	Description	Link
AR school-wide examples	Review of one school's AR processes from initial planning, implementation, and results.	https://www.edutopia.org/article/how-teachers-can-learn-through-action-research/
DDDM overview	Discussion of *Making Sense of Data-Driven Decision-Making in Education*, a publication by the Rand Corporation.	https://www.rand.org/pubs/occasional_papers/OP170.html

REFLECTION QUESTIONS

1. Describe the similarities and differences between traditional research and action research.
2. Name and describe the four components of DDDM.
3. Describe the current opportunities within your school to participate in DDDM and action research within various school-based teams.
4. What processes and resources are available to you and your colleagues to conduct DDDM on various teams?
5. As you consider the various opportunities to use DDDM skills, what current opportunities could be used by you and your colleagues to begin and/or enhance the expert use of DDDM and action research?

REFERENCES

Adelman, C. (1993). Kurt Lewin and the origins of action research. *Educational Action Researchers, 1*(1), 7–25.

Anfara, V. A., and Mertz, N. T. (2015). *Theoretical framework in qualitative research*. Second edition. Thousand Oaks, CA: Sage.

Calhoun, E. F. (1994). *How to use action research in the self-renewing school*. Alexandria, VA: Association for Supervision and Curriculum Development.

Cook, B. G., and Odom, S. L. (2013). Evidence-based practices and implementation science in special education. *Exceptional children, 79*(2), 135–44.

Creswell, J. W. (2013). *Qualitative inquiry and research design: Choosing among five approaches*. Third edition. Thousand Oaks, CA: Sage.

Elliott, S. 1991. *Action research for educational change*. Bristol, PA: Open University Press.

Every Student Succeeds Act of 2015, Pub. L. No. 114–95 114 § Stat. 117 (2015). https://congress.gov/114/plaws/publ95/PLAW-114publ95.pdf

Gesel, S. A., LeJeune, L. M., Chow, J. C., Sinclair, A. C., and Lemons, C. J. (2021). A meta-analysis of the impact of professional development on teachers' knowledge, skill, and self-efficacy in data-based decision-making. *Journal of Learning Disabilities, 54*(4), 269–83.

Green, J. L., Schmitt-Wilson, S., Versland, T., Kelting-Gibson, L., and Nollmeyer, G. E. (2016). Teachers and data literacy: A blueprint for professional development to foster data driven decision making. *Journal of Continuing Education and Professional Development, 3*(1), 14–32.

Hattie, J. (2012). *Visible learning for teachers: Maximizing impact on learning*. Routledge.

Hoy, W. K. (2016). *Quantitative research: A primer*. Second edition. Thousand Oaks, CA: Sage.

Hubbard, R. S., and Power, B. M. (1999). *Living the questions: A guide for teacher-researchers*. Portland, ME: Stenhouse Publishers.

Johnson, R. B., and Christensen, L. B. (2016). *Educational research: Quantitative, qualitative, and mixed approaches*. Sixth edition. Thousand Oaks, CA: Sage.

Lewin, K. (1952). Group decision and social change. In G. E. Swanson, T. M. Newcomb, and E. L. Hartley (Eds.), *Readings in social psychology*. New York: Holt.

Mertler, C. (2020). *Action research: Improving schools and empowering educators*. New York: Sage.

Muñoz, M. A., and Guskey, T. R. (2015). Standards-based grading and reporting will improve education. *Phi Delta Kappan, 96*(7), 64–68.

Poortman, C. L., and Schildkamp, K. (2016). Solving student achievement problems with a data use intervention for teachers. *Teaching and Teacher Education, 60*, 425–33. https://doi.org/10.1016/j.tate.2016.06.010

Schmuck, R. A. (1997). *Practical action research for change*. Arlington Heights, IL: IRI SkyLight Training and Publishing, Inc.

Chapter Two

Equity-Based Action Research

INTRODUCTION

This chapter emphasizes the critical need for educators to be culturally competent and culturally relevant in their approaches to action research in their classrooms and in their schools. This chapter will focus on how equity must be at the foundation of all educational decision-making, including the action research (AR) process. A large focus of this equity-based approach includes the use of culturally relevant assessments, evidence-based strategies, and interventions to meet the needs of *all* students, including those from culturally and linguistically diverse (CLD) backgrounds. Action research is described in culturally responsive and equitable ways, including engaging parents and family members in the process. Topics include information about culturally responsive, relevant, and sustaining teaching approaches; equitable approaches to action research, including appropriate AR approaches and assessment considerations; and building collaborative partnerships. This chapter provides information, strategies, and resources for educators to meet the academic and behavioral needs of CLD students within their daily decisions regarding instruction and assessment.

OBJECTIVES

After reading this chapter, the reader will be able to

- identify asset-based pedagogies and how to apply these to action research;
- recognize the effects of race, language, ethnicity, socioeconomic status, and other markers of difference on research practice and results;
- analyze the need for accommodating and modifying assessment, instruction, and materials to meet individual student's needs, including those who are CLD;
- embrace the importance of creating positive working relationships with parents and family members of students from diverse backgrounds; and
- identify strategies and resources to meet the academic and behavioral needs of CLD students in instruction and assessment.

KEY TERMS

Intersectionality: The ways in which systems of inequality based on gender, race, ethnicity, sexual orientation, gender identity, disability, class, and other forms of discrimination "intersect," creating unique dynamics and effects.

Culturally responsive teaching: Using students' customs, characteristics, experiences, and perspectives as tools for better classroom instruction.

Culturally relevant pedagogy: A theoretical model that focuses on multiple aspects of student achievement and supports students to uphold their cultural identities and calls for students to develop critical perspectives that challenge societal inequities.

Culturally sustaining pedagogy: A strengths-based instructional approach that centers and sustains the cultural and linguistic identities, experiences, and ways of knowing of diverse students, families/caregivers, and communities.

Culturally and linguistically diverse (CLD): A broad term used to describe communities or individuals whose races, ethnic backgrounds, languages, and other cultural factors differ from the culture of power.

Minoritized: Individuals or groups who have been made subordinate in status to a more dominant group or its members.

Marginalized: The act of treating a person or group as though they are insignificant by isolating and/or disempowering them. The term "marginalized" describes the person or group that is being treated insignificantly, pushed to the margins of society, and rendered powerless.

Critical consciousness decision-making (CCDM) model: This model, created by Broughton and colleagues (2022), provides education professionals with a reflective process across six stages for engaging in the IEP process with a language-as-resource stance, regardless of background or training in bilingual education.

Equitable education: Education that provides students with resources that fit their circumstances, providing students with what they need in order to be successful.

Implicit bias: Automatic and unconscious stereotypes, often shaping how people behave and make decisions without their awareness that they are doing so.

Explicit bias: When one is aware of their preexisting beliefs or stereotypes about a specific group of people and makes intentional decisions based on these beliefs.

VIGNETTE

Ms. Hernandez has been using action research to evaluate the progress of all students in her class and a trend she is noticing is that her students from CLD backgrounds are scoring lower on average on many of her assessment measures than their White classmates. In daily interactions with her CLD students, she knows them to be competent in the subject matter and successfully participate in class discussions and activities, but in formal data collection, they seem to underperform. She began to question what may be occurring in the types of assessment that her school district and state require that don't seem to capture the true ability of certain groups of students. Is there something different she should be doing in her instruction? In her assessment?

INCREASING DIVERSITY AND INEQUITABLE EXPERIENCES

Students from diverse backgrounds are often referred to as culturally and linguistically diverse (CLD). The term "CLD" generally refers to students who come from various minoritized backgrounds such as racial or ethnic minorities (for example, Black, Hispanic, Indigenous), multilingual learners (MLs), students living in poverty, and students who come from immigrant/refugee backgrounds. The term "minoritized" is used in this chapter rather than "minorities" because it better highlights the active processes that structural racism has had in holding certain groups out of the mainstream population. As mentioned in the introduction of this book, US schools are becoming increasingly diverse in their racial, ethnic, linguistic, and cultural compositions. White, non-Hispanic students currently comprise only 45 percent of the public school population (Irwin et al., 2023). Cultural statuses such as social class, gender and sexual orientation, religion, and ability level are so diverse among today's learners that it may be difficult to describe what represents a "typical learner." As such, the term "minority," which refers to the smaller number, is not applicable to CLD learners who now actually make up the majority of students in schools yet still remain minoritized in status.

Students from CLD backgrounds often face additional challenges in learning and demonstrating what they have learned. In fact, the United States has a long and well-documented history of educational inequities for students from CLD backgrounds that have led to disproportionate representation in special education programs, disproportionate exclusionary disciplinary practices, and higher rates of school dropout for CLD learners (Artiles et al., 2013; Avant, 2016). The outcomes are even more dire for students from CLD backgrounds who have also been identified with disabilities; CLD students with disabilities are even more susceptible to facing challenges in being successful in school settings (Faircloth et al., 2016).

Dr. Kimberlé Crenshaw coined the term "intersectionality" in 1989 to describe the experience of living with multiple minoritized identities. Minoritized identities may include those around gender, race, culture, disability, gender identity, sexual orientation, immigration status, and others. In fact, the feeling of being minoritized is often in the eye of the person who is feeling "othered." For CLD students, the overlap of these varying identities, particularly having multiple identities that marginalize them (for example, multilingualism, disability, low socioeconomic status, immigration status), puts them at the greatest risk for identification and placement in special education, more segregated and restrictive settings once placed, and poorer long-term outcomes within schools and beyond (Cramer et al., 2023). In this chapter, we use the term "marginalized" to capture the experience of CLD learners, including those with disabilities, who have been pushed aside and excluded or isolated from mainstream society through power imbalances (Causadias and Umaña-Taylor, 2018).

> **READ MORE ABOUT IT!**
>
> Learn more about the Institute of Education Sciences and the equity standards at https://ies.ed.gov/ncer/whatsnew/techworkinggroup/pdf/TASEBUEquityTWG.pdf.

Due to the intersectionality of race, special education, and exclusionary practices, many students of color, multilinguals, youth living in poverty, and students with disabilities face disparate and restrictive practices that deny them access to an appropriate education (Connor et al., 2019), causing students additional challenges in learning and demonstrating what they have learned. Many researchers believe that these additional challenges are a product of unequally structured learning opportunities (for example, Avant, 2016), such as lower teacher expectations, cultural differences in students' and teachers' behavioral expectations, language differences, and poverty (Harry and Klingner, 2022). Due to this long history of inequities in educational experiences, CLD students as a group consistently face challenges in academic, psychosocial, and behavioral outcomes (Office of Special Education Programs, 2021). To remediate this, it is important that educators create spaces where all students feel included, welcome, and respected. When designing and implementing action research projects, it is critical to consider the varying identities of students in the classroom and ensure that equitable curriculum, assessment, and interventions are in place to address issues of bias, discrimination, and oppression.

> Stop and Reflect:
>
> What do you think may be some causes of the negative educational outcomes for students from minoritized backgrounds?
>
> What are some things you may try to do differently with your students to improve outcomes for CLD learners?

FEDERAL APPROACHES TO EQUITABLE EDUCATION

Multiple federal regulations have been mandated over the past twenty-five years to address these well-documented educational disparities. Part of these mandates includes using systematic procedures for screening, intervening, and monitoring students demonstrating deficits before making evaluation decisions for disability placement (National Center for Learning Disabilities, 2011). In response, multi-tiered systems of supports (MTSS) frameworks, such as response to intervention and positive behavioral interventions and supports (PBIS) have been widely adopted in schools to meet these mandates and attempt to reduce inappropriate disability diagnosis. These frameworks will be discussed in more detail in chapter 4. While the use of MTSS can certainly remove some bias from educational processes, recent studies demonstrate that many educators feel unprepared to implement MTSS with fidelity, causing professionals to lean on their cultural values and often leading to misinterpretations of CLD students' behaviors (Avant, 2016; Sabnis et al., 2020). Further, MTSS is used inconsistently across states, districts, and schools, making it difficult to pinpoint effective MTSS approaches for CLD students (Balu et al., 2015; Cramer, 2015).

A recent consensus report of the National Academies of Sciences, Engineering, and Medicine (2022) called for the advancement of "equity-oriented science" in education research. Following this, the Institute of Educational Sciences, the statistics, research, and evaluation arm of the US Department of Education, introduced a new equity standard and associated recommendations around equity to its Standards for Excellence in Education Research. This new standard reads, "Researchers who are designing and testing interventions must clearly demonstrate how those interventions address education inequities, such as by improving learners' outcomes and/or their access to resources and opportunities" (NASEM, 2022, p. 4). In the same year, a working group was formed to determine what additional resources and supports might be necessary for researchers to integrate a focus on equity into educational interventions. As educators, the same focus on integrating equity into classroom instruction, interventions, and DDDM must be considered.

CULTURALLY RESPONSIVE, RELEVANT, AND SUSTAINING APPROACHES

One of the most important things that educators can do to integrate equity into their classrooms is to abandon deficit thinking and low expectations for their diverse learners. Three main asset-based approaches have been recommended to provide equitable instruction for CLD learners: culturally responsive teaching (Gay, 2018), culturally relevant pedagogy (Ladson-Billings, 2021), and culturally sustaining pedagogy (Paris and Alim, 2017).

Culturally Responsive Teaching

"Culturally responsive teaching" is a term first coined by Geneva Gay in 2000 to describe "using the cultural knowledge, prior experiences, frames of reference and performance styles of ethnically diverse students to make learning encounters more relevant to and effective for them" (Gay, 2010, p. 31). Gay believes that academic knowledge and skills should be connected to students' lived experiences and frames of reference. Because there are often strong cultural variations between the home culture and school culture for CLD students, these real-world connections would make school more meaningful to students and assist in learning and motivation.

Gay's more recent work (2018) continues to offer suggestions for "reversing the underachievement of students of color" (p. 1). Five essential components of culturally responsive teaching that can be applied to action research include (a) having a strong knowledge base about cultural diversity, (b) culturally relevant curricula, (c) high expectations for all students, (d) appreciation for different communication styles, and (e) using multicultural instructional examples. By incorporating these components, teachers can use students' cultural knowledge, experiences, practices, and perspectives to engage them in instruction; bridge gaps between home and school practices; identify and leverage students' strengths to transform education; and provide an education to the whole child. Teachers should also engage in critically questioning normative schooling practices, content, and assessments (Gay, 2018). Tenets of culturally responsive teaching will be infused into recommendations in the remainder of this chapter.

Culturally Relevant Pedagogy

In 1995, Gloria Ladson-Billings studied effective teachers of Black students and used those teachers' beliefs and practices to form a framework of culturally relevant pedagogy, which she defined as a model that "not only addresses student achievement but also helps students to accept and affirm their cultural identity while developing critical perspectives that challenge inequities that schools (and other institutions) perpetuate" (p. 465). The culturally relevant pedagogy framework is one of the most popular asset-based frameworks still used today to guide instruction for CLD learners. The three main components of culturally relevant pedagogy include (a) student learning: prioritizing students' intellectual growth, including their ability to problem solve; (b) cultural competence: creating an environment where students affirm and appreciate their culture of origin while also developing fluency in at least one other culture; and (c) sociopolitical/critical consciousness: teaching students how to identify, analyze, and solve real-world problems, particularly those that result in societal inequities against marginalized groups (Ladson-Billings, 2021).

Similarities may be noted across culturally responsive teaching and culturally relevant pedagogy. Both require teachers to have an understanding of themselves and their own identities as well as an understanding of the cultural values and strengths of their students. Both rely on teachers believing in and expecting all students to produce high-quality work. Both rely on connections to real-world and relevant problem-solving skills. Most recently, researchers have called for theories to go beyond simply maintaining students' heritage and community practices while gaining access to dominant practices. As a response to this call, culturally sustaining pedagogy evolved.

Culturally Sustaining Pedagogy

In 2012, Django Paris expanded on culturally responsive teaching by creating a framework for culturally sustaining pedagogy. This is a strengths-based instructional approach that centers and sustains the cultural and linguistic identities, experiences, and ways of knowing of diverse students, families/caregivers, and communities. Paris asserted that US public schools continue to hold cultural norms that differ from the increasingly multiethnic population of students and that previous asset-based pedagogies (that is, culturally relevant pedagogy and culturally responsive teaching) are insufficient to maintain and value the many cultures in today's schools. Culturally sustaining pedagogy calls for educators to move beyond relevance and responsiveness by exploring how ideas of traditional heritage (for example, traditional dances, clothes, or food) merge with contemporary heritage (for example, hip-hop culture), and how these may show up in and across groups of students (for example, hip-hop culture being as important to Mexican American students as their own home language). Further, this model helps educators understand that culture is fluid and ever changing, whereas former theories on multicultural education often compartmentalize different beliefs and issues as belonging to certain groups of students (Paris and Alim, 2014).

Stop and Reflect:

How does each of the asset-based pedagogies described in this section contribute to providing equity in education?

What are some things you have already been doing in your teaching that may reflect culturally responsive, relevant, or sustaining practices?

What are some new ways you may try to ensure that students' cultures are sustained and valued within your curriculum, instruction, and assessment?

CULTURALLY SUSTAINING ACTION RESEARCH

As you move forward in utilizing action research to inform and guide your instruction, think about how you may apply asset-based pedagogies to ensure that you are providing equitable instruction and assessment procedures for all learners. Some practical suggestions for the successful teaching of students from CLD backgrounds from Polloway and colleagues (2022) suggest that teachers should

- use ongoing and varied assessment as an integral part of instruction (the teacher knows exactly what each student is learning on any given day),
- ensure respectful activities for all the students in their classroom,
- use student differences as a basis for instructional planning,
- measure student growth based on each student's baseline skills,
- provide a wide variety of materials and activities, and
- understand that a student's literacy in her or his first language can be used to help bridge learning for the student to develop literacy in English.

The Council for Exceptional Children released recommendations for high-leverage practices (HLPs) in special education (McLeskey et al., 2017). HLP 7 suggests that teachers should create learning environments that "build mutually respectful relationship with students and engages them in setting classroom climate, be respectful, and value ethnic, cultural, contextual, and linguistic diversity to foster student engagement across learning environments" (p. 20). In applying best practices to action research, these principles can be applied across each step of the action research process. As a reminder from chapter 1, the steps of the action research process include:

- Identify: Use data to identify classroom or school-based area of need.
- Develop and Implement: In response to the data, develop and implement an intervention plan using evidence-based practices.
- Collect and Analyze: After sufficient time, collect assessment data to determine results from the intervention.
- Reflect and Share: After analyzing the data, reflect and share results, taking actions as decided.

To ensure that action research is completed in an equitable fashion, there are steps educators can take at each stage of the process to be intentional about cultural sustainment. In identifying areas of concern, educators should ensure that the needs of all learners are being considered and recognize that not every student's needs are the same. In developing and implementing intervention plans, the types of evidence-based practices selected should be vetted to consider on whom these interventions were vetted. In collecting and analyzing data, educators should examine their collection and assessment methods to ensure that a variety of opportunities and modalities are available for students to demonstrate learning. Have I allowed enough time for students to show growth, and am I in touch with what this growth may look like? Reflection on this process is a key component, however, educators should use this reflection to consider if they have considered the whole child in this process. Table 2.1 provides some important questions for educators to reflect upon as well of examples of how these reflections may be implemented.

At the heart of equitable action research is a classroom in which daily instruction is equitable and of high quality. Culturally sustaining supports that take into account

Table 2.1. Educator Reflections for Culturally Sustaining Action Research Approaches

Reflective Question	Description/Example
Am I choosing assessments that are nonbiased and culturally appropriate for the student whom I am assessing?	Assessments such as these would be in the student's primary language. Assessments would be free from questions that measure student's prior exposure to experiences rather than actual knowledge or performance.
Are evidence-based strategies I am using based on evidence that was studied with a diverse population of students including students from similar backgrounds to my student? Has this strategy been found to be effective for CLD learners?	Consider reviewing literature on evidence-based strategies to determine if there is an evidence base for effectiveness with CLD learners. Utilize websites such as https://crehub.org to search for strategies to use.
Is the intervention that I am using one that has any connections to life of the student for whom I am intervening?	Consider the lived experiences of your students and tie in examples or stories that are relatable for your students. Consider experiential learning experiences.
Am I using nonbiased data to inform my decisions? Am I taking into account the lived experiences of my students and not making assumptions or changing my expectations to guide the process? Am I considering the specific student for whom I am making the decision?	Consider what implicit biases or judgments you may hold that may be informing your decision-making. Make an intentional effort to consider a holistic view using data as objectively as possible.
Am I involving diverse stakeholders in this action research process, including families?	Ensure that you seek out multiple sources of data/points of view. Include parents and families as data sources via parental input forms. Ensure that any multidisciplinary teams are made up of a diverse group of professionals.

the diverse needs of all learners should be an ongoing component of general class instruction and at the foundation of all instruction. In such an environment, typically marginalized students are at the center of the instructional process and educators learn *from* their students rather than simply *about* their students. Students' various and complex intersecting identities are considered across all educational decisions with a goal of increasing academic and behavioral outcomes of students from CLD backgrounds, including those with disabilities. Consideration of the whole child, including socio-emotional supports, is of the utmost importance as this may be necessary to mitigate years of educational inequities and discrepancies.

CULTURALLY SUSTAINING EVIDENCE-BASED PRACTICES AND INTERVENTIONS

Culturally responsive evidence-based practices (Aronson and Laughter, 2016) are critical to the success of equity-based intervention at tier 1. Culturally responsive educators view students' cultural identities (for example, language use, communication style) and contextual experiences as valuable resources for learning. These teachers value the cultural capital that students bring to the table from their lived experiences and use it to build upon and, ultimately, scaffold instruction. In applying culturally sustaining practices, educators apply interactive, collaborative teaching methods that support students' cultural, linguistic, and racial experiences (Ladson-Billings, 2014) and integrate these methods with practices that have been shown to be effective by an established evidence base. These practices consist of approaches including collaborative teaching, responsive feedback, and child-centered instruction (Aceves and Orosco, 2014). Student choice and engagement are integral components of such classrooms. In planning, educators should ask themselves what their lesson has to do with the lives of each of their students. They should ensure they are providing opportunities for choice in classroom activities, encouraging child-directed learning, and assisting students as they engage in these activities. Additionally, equity-focused educators create opportunities for students to demonstrate leadership and autonomy over their learning.

> Stop and Reflect:
>
> Think about a lesson plan you have created. Consider if you have thought about how your lesson is related to the lived experiences of the various students who would be participating in that lesson. Is there room for improvement to ensure that multiple students can connect with your lesson and build on their own experiences to be engaged participants? What are some ways you might be able to refocus instruction to give back more choice and autonomy to the diverse group of learners you have taught or may ultimately teach?

COLLABORATION AND PARTNERSHIPS WITH DIVERSE FAMILIES

At the heart of equity-based recommendations, particularly for CLD learners, is involving parents in their child's education. For example, Broughton and colleagues (2023) provide the critical consciousness decision-making (CCDM) model to guide special education practitioners and IEP teams to use critical consciousness of sociolinguistic and learning factors to make educational decisions for MLs with disabilities. This six-step model includes reflect, review, recognize, plan for service delivery, partner with families and communities, and practice and advocate. Step five focuses on partnering with and engaging families in the special education process. This process includes the student, their family, and relevant community members working together with school personnel to design a wraparound set of services that addresses the strengths and needs identified by the students' holistic profile. Stansberry Brusnahan and colleagues (2023) provide a framework to center equity in education, and a pivotal component of their framework is including diverse student and family input in educational planning. They recommend a participatory policy approach. In this approach, students and families work alongside school personnel participating in decision-making that impacts students' interests, rights, and needs. In Cramer and colleagues' (2023) framework for equity-based MTSS, the authors call for parents and families to be included as critical and valued members of the MTSS process. The Council for Exceptional Children's HLP 3 specifically addresses collaborating with families and in doing so "considering the background, socioeconomic states, language, culture and priorities of the family" (McLeskey et al., 2017, p. 18).

Families are arguably the most critical stakeholders for CLD students, and family collaboration is an integral part of equity-based action research. Student success is tremendously enhanced when practices are reinforced at home, so schools should strive to maintain collaborative and valuable relationships across MTSS tiers and consider the input of extended family members in the child's life in DDDM. The input of families should also be considered to create a family-school partnership that enforces consistency of expectations across the home and school environments as well as buy-in for parents and students alike (Szech, 2021). When educators value the input of parents and recognize them as equal partners with valuable perspectives, students' cultures are sustained and respected (Garbacz et al., 2017). Rossetti and colleagues (2017) stated that culturally responsive collaboration is the key element in collaboration with CLD families of students with disabilities and provide three guiding questions for school personnel to consider. First, personnel reflect on "How culturally responsive am I?" Next, they consider, "Who is this family?" Finally, they consider, "Have we developed a collaborative partnership?" To involve families in the action research process, educators can take the following steps:

- Reflect on your own ability to be a culturally responsive collaborator.
- Take the time to get to know the families of your students and demonstrate your value and respect for the child and the family.

- Seek input from the family regarding what goals may be important to focus on across domains of academics, behavior, and socioemotional well-being.
- Include families as collaborators in the action research process. Let them provide sources of data based on what they are observing at home and in the community.
- Share results you are finding so they know what is and isn't working. This will allow them to carry over effective practices at home.

Stop and Reflect:

In the vignette, Ms. Hernandez is observing discrepancies between the performance of her students from CLD backgrounds and her other students. Her CLD students are scoring lower on average on many of her assessment measures compared to their White classmates. Now that you have been provided with information about systemic and implicit biases that have existed and learned about asset-based pedagogies, consider some suggestions you may have to offer Ms. Hernandez about ways she can adjust her instruction and evaluation to better reach her students and more accurately evaluate their learning.

SUMMARY

Although US schools have become increasingly diverse, students from CLD backgrounds have continued to face systemic inequities in accessing educational opportunities. Researchers have suggested asset-based pedagogies as a shift for how educators can ensure that all learners are engaged in instruction that affirms their culture and focuses on the diverse and nuanced needs of learners from marginalized groups. These and other intentional shifts place equity at the foundation of all educational decision-making, including in the action research process. Through self-reflection, careful and intentional planning, and collaborative partnerships, educators can move toward equitable decision-making and instruction for all learners.

KEY TAKEAWAYS

Subjective decision-making has historically undermined children from CLD backgrounds.

Culturally sustaining practices focus on the assets that children from all backgrounds bring to their classrooms and allow children and their lived experiences to guide classroom practices.

Equitable foundations in MTSS and DDDM require reflection and intentionality to ensure educators are not relying on implicit biases to inform their decisions.

Families are a key and valuable partner in equitable action research processes.

Instruction and assessment practices must be inclusive of all learners and incorporate equitable approaches.

Where can I find more information about equity-based action research?

Resource	Description	Link
Culturally and Linguistically Responsive MTSS for Multilingual Students	This comprehensive PowerPoint details culturally and linguistically responsive MTSS for multilingual students and references model demonstration research funded by OSEP.	https://ncela.ed.gov/files/uploads/2017/Culturally_and_Linguistically-Slide_View.pdf
Culturally Responsive Education (CRE) Hub	CRE Hub provides the history, tools, and resources to contextualize and build the movement for culturally responsive education and ethnic studies.	https://crehub.org/
Culturally Responsive PBIS	CRPBIS is an educational initiative grounded in local to global justice theory. Local schools collaborate with communities to engage in research. This site highlights Bal's collaborative and inclusive problem-solving research and Learning Labs.	http://www.crpbis.org
Culturally Responsive Teaching Guide	This publication serves as a guide to implementing culturally responsive teaching practices. It offers research-based, high-quality strategies that highlight best practice skills for teaching all students equitably.	https://educationnorthwest.org/sites/default/files/resources/culturally-responsive-teaching-508.pdf
IRIS Center Module on Culturally and Linguistically Diverse Learners	This module examines the ways in which culture influences the daily interactions that occur across all classrooms and provides practice for enhancing culturally responsive teaching.	https://iris.peabody.vanderbilt.edu/module/clde/#content
PBIS Cultural Responsiveness Field Guide	This field guide is part of a five-point intervention approach for enhancing equity in student outcomes within a schoolwide positive behavioral interventions and supports (SWPBIS) approach by aligning culturally responsive practices to the core components of SWPBIS. The goal of using this guide is to make school systems more responsive to the cultures and communities that they serve.	https://www.pbis.org/resource/pbis-cultural-responsiveness-field-guide-resources-for-trainers-and-coaches

REFLECTION QUESTIONS

1. Describe some potential reasons that CLD learners have faced negative educational outcomes.
2. Compare the different asset-based pedagogies (that is, culturally responsive teaching, culturally relevant pedagogy, and culturally sustaining pedagogy). Which of these do you feel would be most effective for you to use in your classroom?
3. How can equitable action research practices lead to improved educational experiences for CLD learners?
4. How will you ensure that your action research processes consider diverse learners in your classroom or school?
5. How might you involve families in your action research efforts?

REFERENCES

Aceves, T. C., and Orosco, M. J. (2014). Culturally responsive teaching (Document No. IC-2). University of Florida, Collaboration for Effective Educator, Development, Accountability, and Reform Center website, http://ceedar.education.ufl.edu/tools/innovation-configurations/

Aronson, B., and Laughter, J. (2016). The theory and practice of culturally relevant education: A synthesis of research across content areas. *Review of Educational Research, 86*(1), 163–206. https://doi.org/10.3102/0034654315582066

Artiles, A. J. (2013). Untangling the racialization of disabilities: An intersectionality critique across disability models. *Du Bois Review: Social Science Research on Race, 10*(2), 329–47.

Avant, D. W. (2016). Using response to intervention/multi-tiered systems of supports to promote social justice in schools. *Journal for Multicultural Education, 10*(4), 507–20. https://doi.org/10.1108/jme-06-2015-0019

Balu, R., Zhu, P., Doolittle, F., Schiller, E., Jenkins, J., and Gersten, R. (2015). Evaluation of response to intervention practices for elementary school reading. NCEE 2016-4000. *National Center for Education Evaluation and Regional Assistance*.

Broughton, A. J., Przymus, S. D., Ortiz, A. A., and Cruz, B. J. S. (2023). Critical consciousness in decision-making: A model for educational planning and instruction with bilingual/multi lingual students with disabilities. *Teaching Exceptional Children, 55*(5), 338–49. https://doi.org/10.1177/00400599221093655

Causadias, J. M., and Umaña-Taylor, A. J. (2018). Reframing marginalization and youth development: Introduction to the special issue. *American Psychologist, 73*(6), 707.

Choi, J., McCart, A., and Sailor, W. Reshaping educational policies for inclusive education. *Research in Education, 6*(1). https://doi.org/10.32865/fire202061179

Connor, D., Cavendish, W., Gonzalez, T., and Jean-Pierre, P. (2019). Is a bridge even possible over troubled waters? The field of special education negates the overrepresentation of minority students: A DisCrit analysis. *Race Ethnicity and Education, 22*(6), 723–45.

Cramer, E. D. (2015). Inequities of intervention among culturally and linguistically diverse students. *Perspectives on Urban Education Journal, 12*(1).

Cramer, E. D., Theodore, S., Lumpkins, A., Cummings, C. S., and Flores, H. (2023). Enhancing social justice via equity-based multi-tiered systems of supports. In J. Chityo and Z. Pietrantoni (Eds.), *Social justice and culturally affirming education in K–12 settings* (pp. 111–32). IGI Global. https://doi.org/10.4018/978-1-6684-6386-4.ch006

Crenshaw, K. (1989). Demarginalizing the intersection of race and sex: A Black feminist critique of antidiscrimination doctrine. University of Chicago Legal Forum, 139–168.

Faircloth, S., Toldson, I., and Lucio, R. (2016). Decreasing dropout rates for minority male youth with disabilities from culturally and ethnically diverse backgrounds. National Dropout Prevention Center for Students with Disabilities. http://www.ndpc-sd.org/documents/EDC-2014-monograph-book.pdf

Garbacz, S. A., Herman, K. C., Thompson, A. M., and Reinke, W. M. (2017). Family engagement in education and intervention: Implementation and evaluation to maximize family, school, and student outcomes. *Journal of School Psychology, 62*, 1–10. https://doi.org/10.1016/j.jsp.2017.04.002

Gay, G. (2018). *Culturally responsive teaching: Theory, research, and practice.* Third edition. Teachers College Press.

Gay, G. (2010). Culturally responsive teaching: Theory, research, and practice. Second edition. Multicultural education series. Teachers College Press.

Gay, G. (2002). Preparing for culturally responsive teaching. *Journal of Teacher Education, 53*(2), 106–16.

Harry, B., and Klingner, J. (2022). *Why are so many students of color in special education?: Understanding race and disability in schools.* Teachers College Press.

Irwin, V., Wang, K., Tezil, T., Zhang, J., Filbey, A., Jung, J., Bullock Mann, F., Dilig, R., and Parker, S. (2023). Report on the condition of education 2023 (NCES 2023-144rev). US Department of Education. National Center for Education Statistics. https://nces.ed.gov/pubsearch/pubsinfo.asp?pubid=2023144rev

Ladson-Billings, G. (1995). Toward a theory of culturally relevant pedagogy. *American Educational Research Journal, 32*(3), 465–91. https://doi.org/10.3102/00028312032003465

Ladson-Billings, G. (2014). Culturally relevant pedagogy 2.0: Aka the remix. *Harvard Educational Review, 84*(1), 74–84. https://doi.org/10.3102/00028312032003465

Ladson-Billings, G. (2021). *Culturally relevant pedagogy: Asking a different question.* Teachers College Press.

McLeskey, J., Council for Exceptional Children, and Collaboration for Effective Educator Development, Accountability and Reform. (2017). High-leverage practices in special education. Council for Exceptional Children.

National Academies of Sciences, Engineering, and Medicine (NASEM) (2022). The future of education research at IES: Advancing an equity-oriented science. The National Academies Press. https://doi.org/10.17226/26428

National Center for Learning Disabilities. (2011). Multi-tier system of supports aka response to intervention (RTI). https://www.ncld.org/wp-content/uploads/2011/05/MTSS-brief-in-LJ-template.pdf

Office of Special Education Programs. (2021). Individuals with Disabilities Education Act (IDEA) database. US Department of Education. https://www2.ed.gov/programs/osepidea/618-data/state-level-datafiles/index.html#bcc

Paris, D. (2012). Culturally sustaining pedagogy: A needed change in stance, terminology, and practice. *Educational Researcher, 41*(3), 93–97. https://doi.org/10.3102/0013189X12441244

Paris, D., and Alim, H. S. (2014). What are we seeking to sustain through culturally sustaining pedagogy? A loving critique forward. *Harvard Educational Review, 84*(1), 85–100. https://doi.org/10.17763/haer.84.1.982l873k2ht16m77

Paris, D., and Alim, H. S. (Eds.). (2017). *Culturally sustaining pedagogies: Teaching and learning for justice in a changing world.* Teachers College Press.

Polloway, E. A., Patton, J. R., Serna, L., and Bailey, J. W. (2022). *Strategies for teaching learners with special needs.* Twelfth edition. Pearson.

Rossetti, Z., Sauer, J. S., Bui, O., and Ou, S. (2017). Developing collaborative partnerships with culturally and linguistically diverse families during the IEP process. *Teaching Exceptional Children, 49*(5), 328–38.

Sabnis, S., Castillo, J. M., and Wolgemuth, J. R. (2020). RTI, equity, and the return to the status quo: Implications for consultants. *Journal of Educational and Psychological Consultation, 30*(3), 285–313.

Szech, L. (2021). How the funds of knowledge theory shifted teachers' dominant narratives of family involvement. *School Community Journal, 31*(1), 149–70.

Stansberry Brusnahan, L., Maguire, E., Harkins Monaco, E. A., Leckie, A., Bailey, S., and Fuller, M. (2023). Leading with an equity lens: Addressing the intersection of racism and ableism in public schools. *Teaching Exceptional Children, 55*(5), 302–13. https://doi.org/10.1177/00400599231173073

Chapter Three

Data Collection and Analysis

INTRODUCTION

This chapter focuses on types of assessments, data collection, and analysis. Rationale and descriptions of various assessments, including teacher-made tests, standardized assessments, and observational data, are described for data collection in academic and behavioral settings. Also, practical guidelines and examples are provided for identifying, constructing, using, and understanding data collection assessments. Several templates for data collection, analyses, and reflection are provided.

OBJECTIVES

After reading this chapter, the reader will be able to

- describe various assessments for academics and behavior for use in the data-driven decision-making (DDDM) process,
- determine uses for various assessments within the multi-tiered system of supports (MTSS) and action research (AR) processes, and
- identify sources of assessments for use in the DDDM process.

KEY TERMS

Curriculum-based assessment (CBA): A set of procedures that links assessment directly to instruction and evaluates progress using measures taken from the curricula.

Curriculum-based measures (CBM): An approach to measuring students' academic growth along with evaluating the effectiveness of instruction in the classroom (Deno, 2003). It consists of a simple set of standardized procedures that are a way to obtain reliable and valid measurement of a student's achievement.

Diagnostic assessments: Specific, targeted assessments that provide data to assist educators in designing individualized instruction and intensifying intervention for students who do not respond to validated intervention programs. Diagnostic tools can be either informal, which are easy-to-use tools that can be administered with little training, or standardized, which must be delivered in a standard way by trained staff.

Formative assessments: Assessments aligned to curricular goals to monitor student learning. They provide ongoing feedback that can be used by teachers to improve their teaching and by students to improve their learning. Strengths and weaknesses are identified to target instruction and interventions.

Functional behavioral assessment (FBA): A diagnostic evaluation technique used to determine the function of a student's behavior and the factors that maintain the behavior.

Progress monitoring: Probes to assess students' academic or behavioral performance, to quantify their rates of improvement or progress toward goals, and to determine how students are responding to instruction and/or interventions.

Replacement behavior: Desired behavior that aligns with classroom expectations for student behavior.

Summative assessment: End of unit assessments to evaluate student learning, knowledge, proficiency, or success at the conclusion of an instructional period, such as a unit, course, or program. Summative assessments can be norm referenced, formally graded, and are often a source of accountability.

Target behavior: Behavior of concern exhibited by the student that does not meet the classroom expectations.

Universal screening: Initial assessment data collection and systematic process to identify students who may be at risk for poor learning outcomes, including academic, behavioral, social-emotional, school completion, and college and career readiness outcomes. Screening data can also be used to identify schools that need support due to large numbers of struggling students.

VIGNETTE

During our faculty meeting yesterday, the discussion focused on assessments. We broke into grade-level teams to discuss our thoughts for universal screening, diagnostic assessments, progress monitoring, and summary assessments. We needed to determine what our students know before we begin instruction. I realized that doing so will help me prepare my lessons so that my students learn the content effectively. I can do that! I do understand the importance of assessing my students with universal screening, using the data to work on my lesson planning and delivery, and working with students to achieve mastery of the content. I want to use assessment to assist me in my teaching practices. I do use some assessment practices in my classroom now, but not as frequently as I think I should. I also want to learn how to use different assessments in order to teach all of my students. My goal for this year is to gain a better understanding of all the purposes and types of assessment so I can be much more effective in the classroom.

—Ms. Hernandez

UNDERSTANDING THE PURPOSES AND TYPES OF ASSESSMENT

Assessment is integral to planning and instruction within classrooms. Results of assessments are not only emphasized for accountability purposes but also critical to the planning processes used to inform professional decisions about academic and behavioral instruction and interventions. The use of ongoing, accurate assessments provides teachers, other school-based educators, and parents with information to inform, deliver, and adapt instruction and interventions throughout the teaching and learning process. Teachers analyze the data to adjust instructional practices to improve student learning. In addition, observational and diagnostic assessment data provide information for classroom management and individual behavioral plans and interventions. Examining assessment data influences instructional methods, resources, and approaches determined by teachers within the AR process. This chapter describes various types of assessments to use in the AR process by teachers to improve student learning and performance. Another goal of this chapter is to describe types and uses of assessments to collect data for decision-making within the MTSS framework by teachers and members of the MTSS team. MTSS is a three- or four-tiered instruction, intervention, and DDDM framework that begins with evidence-based instruction for all students. Defining characteristics of MTSS include (a) researched, evidence-based practices at all tiers; (b) DDDM process; and (c) individualized and targeted interventions (Lemons et al., 2017). Chapter 4 describes the definition, components, and connections of curriculum, instruction, and assessments to implement MTSS by teachers and school-based educators.

ASSESSMENTS SHOULD:

- Match what students have been studying.
- Focus on important content rather than trivia.
- Yield useful information, not just "scores."
- Use clear and helpful criteria.
- Provide a complete picture of students' learning and abilities. (NCTM, 2020)

Teachers and other educators must be knowledgeable of and able to articulate goals in relation to the curriculum standards and classroom behavioral expectations. Knowledge and use of various assessments related to DDDM to identify goals is critical. Teachers use the evidence collected from assessments to set specific goals, develop instructional and intervention plans, and continuously monitor the progress and impacts of these decisions. Therefore multiple assessment methods for gathering and using assessment data within the DDDM process are needed to differentiate instruction, identify interventions, and develop data-driven individual academic and behavior plans to promote student success within classrooms. In addition, practical examples of the use of various assessments within classrooms are described. Also, multiple resources of evidenced-based assessments for use with groups and individual students are shared.

Educators use various types of assessments to address needs to collect data for both external and internal purposes. Formal assessments are usually dictated by federal, state, or district policies and mandates. For example, standardized student testing and DDDM were a central focus of the Every Student Succeeds Act legislation of 2015. As a result, standardized student testing occurs annually, and educators are held accountable for student results through mandatory testing programs within states and local school districts. These can include state assessments, district benchmark assessments, and district-selected, norm-referenced tests, such as the Iowa Test of Basic Skills. The purpose of formal assessments is to measure student learning related to local, state, and national norms. It is important to note that formal assessments are usually administered annually and cannot reflect the efficiency of teaching in process. Various high-stakes accountability systems use formal assessment results from state-administered assessments.

Informal assessments, also referred to as formative assessments, deliver assessment results during and throughout the instructional process. Some are used in progress monitoring so that results can inform instructional decisions. Others may be used as ongoing diagnostic tools with the results focused on modification and/or adjustment of our teaching practices. They are usually embedded within the instructional process. Both the teacher and the student use the results to make decisions about what actions to take to promote further learning. This ongoing, dynamic process involves far more frequent testing, and measurement of student learning is just one of its components. For example, a classroom teacher involved in the AR process may collect data while observing student engagement, motivation, and learning within lessons to make decisions regarding adaptations, accommodations, or intensification that may be needed by students.

There are numerous types of assessments to inform instructional decisions during the DDDM process of action research (Kress and Fry, 2016). Assessments may be used in isolation or in combination with others for the purpose of providing important information (Honig et al., 2018). Increased emphasis on using multiple assessments to assess students' learning provides a more in-depth and reliable picture for solution development. Table 3.1 lists a brief description.

Table 3.1. Types of Assessments

Objective	Includes true/false responses, yes/no answers, and multiple-choice questions
Alternative	Includes portfolios, journals, notebooks, projects, and presentations
Authentic	Incorporates real-life functions and applications
Performance	Requires completion of a task, project or investigation, communication of information, or construction of a response
Naturalistic	Observation of students performance and behavior in an informal context
Achievement Test Battery	Subtests of concepts and skills that usually include technical aspects
Standardized	Formal, standardized samples to establish norms and make inferences
Diagnostic	Teacher made or commercially made instructional models to determine additional information

Stop and Reflect:

As you reflect on formal and informal assessments, what types of assessments are you already using in your classroom, school, and district? How do you or how could you use these assessments to implement action research? Also, how could other professionals in your school use assessment information in collaboration with others?

FOUR TYPES OF ASSESSMENTS

The intent of DDDM is to ensure that students receive rich experiences and differentiated instruction to improve learning. Therefore teachers and other educational service providers use multiple sources of assessment data to determine student learning and behavior (Consortium, 2008). This information forms the basis for educators to continuously analyze, revise, and enhance the instruction and determine academic and behavioral interventions within the DDDM process for use by teachers in action research and/or teachers and team members of the MTSS school teams. The four types of assessments that are important within DDDM include universal screening, progress monitoring, diagnostic, and summative assessment. The following sections take a closer look at each of these four types of assessments with definitions, examples, and resources.

Universal Screening

Universal screening assessments collect student performance data that focus on curriculum standards. They provide important preliminary or baseline information about students' previous and current strengths and weaknesses. One source of universal screening data comes from the state and/or district benchmark assessments of mandated curriculum standards. These standardized assessments are provided at the initiation of a school year or the beginning of a unit of study. These screening measures are generally used by district- or school-based administrators and/or instructional coaches as a broad indicator of student knowledge, skills, and abilities for the purpose of program planning for instructional services. For example, often student screening data from mandated state assessments are reported as baseline data for the School Improvement Plan and program planning. In addition, numerous school districts develop and administer multiple benchmark assessments several times a school year that are aligned with the state and district curriculum standards to provide continuous assessment data related to student learning using a standardized assessment measure. Therefore these assessments should also become part of the initial, universal screening assessment data of the instructional DDDM and lesson planning processes by teachers within their classrooms.

These assessment data become an integral part of the teaching and learning process because they provide information about our students' learning aligned to state and district curriculum standards and benchmarks. A review of previous records will provide important assessment information about student skills and competencies, especially if trends or inconsistencies in student learning are noticed. This information will be useful when considering instructional goals, student groups, and necessary resources. The guiding questions in table 3.2 can be used to inform your record review.

Table 3.2. Guiding Questions for Assessment Reviews

Source of Data	Guiding Questions to Consider
Previous standardized test results	• What are the areas of strength? • What are the areas of need? • Are the areas of strength and need consistent? • Are the areas of need in areas that impact performance? • Are the data consistent or do they show a trend with previous years' scores?
Past summative assessments	• Are the summative assessments from prior units of study consistent? • Are results of the summative assessments reflective of performance that is consistent with peers? For instance, did most students do very well or very poorly on a specific assessment?
Universal screening (such as a grade-level assessment)	• Do the screening data reflect consistencies with the standardized test data? • Are there areas that seem to be consistent? • Are there areas that are not consistent? • What specific content standards appear to be areas of strength and areas of additional instruction?

Progress Monitoring

The goal of progress monitoring is to increase student achievement and growth by making informed educational decisions regarding individual students based upon continuously collected assessment data. Progress monitoring is a foundation for other educational practices in a DDDM process. Once assessment data have been collected, reviewed, and used to develop academic and behavioral goals for instruction and interventions, progress monitoring assessments are used to provide continuous feedback to educators and members of the MTSS team. When progress monitoring is used effectively, teachers continuously revisit academic and behavioral decisions about each student's instructional plan through action research. Teachers will know which students are succeeding and which students need additional interventions and/or additional services. Student achievement and growth are increased as academic and behavioral plans become more individualized and differentiated based on data within each of the three tiers of the MTSS framework (Gesel et al., 2020).

Progress monitoring assessments are usually short and frequent skill-based assessments that provide a snapshot of student learning related to the instructional objective. Often progress-monitoring probes may be the same or similar to initial data collection assessments as described in the previous section and can be used to collect data related to academic goals or behavioral expectations. In addition, instructionally relevant assessment data are from broad categories for progress monitoring instruments and can include

- published program assessments (in conjunction with published curriculum programs),
- published content assessments/inventories,
- informal teacher-created assessments that align with predetermined benchmarks or student's individual prior performance, and
- curriculum-based measurements (CBM) measuring a specific skill in the content areas aligned with curriculum benchmarks.

Table 3.3. Guiding Questions—Curriculum-Based Measures

Source of Data	Guiding Questions to Consider
Curriculum-based measures	• Does this formative assessment align with state and district standards and benchmarks? • Does the curriculum have assessments available? • Were student results consistent with other assessments? • What are the areas of strength? • What are the areas of need? • How will I use this information when planning for instruction?

Diagnostic Assessment in Academics

The purpose of diagnostic assessments is to evaluate the underlying knowledge and skills of individual students related to the specific learning goal. Diagnostic assessment data provides additional and specific information regarding skills and abilities to target intense intervention. Teachers and other instructional personnel (for example, interventionists, instructional coaches) use these results within the solution-finding processes of DDDM within the MTSS framework to meet more individualized student needs (National Center on Intensive Intervention, n.d.). Diagnostic assessment often focuses on one area or domain of knowledge and can be administered before and/or during instruction within a school or classroom setting. For example, diagnostic assessments may be administered throughout a school or grade level specifically targeting necessary prerequisite skills of fifth-grade students during the first week of instruction. The results determine specific, necessary knowledge and skills to build on for curricular content. In addition, a teacher may administer a diagnostic assessment to check for student understanding and/or to correct for misunderstandings. The use of diagnostic assessments identifies students who are experiencing problems at an early stage to plan appropriate instruction and/or interventions. Data collected during classroom observations record student performance information as well. See figure 3.1 for several example templates.

During instruction, the data from formative, diagnostic assessments provide teachers with more in-depth and specific information of the strengths and/or deficits of individual students related to curriculum goals. For example, specific work samples of individual students can be reviewed to identify error patterns, deficits in conceptual understandings, and/or other concerns with conceptual understandings to better identify specific skill deficits in prior knowledge. This type of analysis also indicates the student's strengths, and the results can be used by the teacher in lesson planning, providing differentiated instruction, and identifying needed interventions.

To use diagnostic assessment methods effectively in the classroom, feedback to students is critical. This should be done often to ensure students recognize areas of need or to correct error patterns and misconceptions. One-to-one and small group discussions with the students provide opportunities to correct misunderstandings in conceptual understanding by exploring why answers are right or wrong. This information from diagnostic teaching and diagnostic assessment provides important understanding and information to better individualize instruction and interventions for struggling students (Mason and Smith, 2020).

Notes

Name: Susan		
Date	Anecdote	Action
11/15	Susan was able to identify rhyming pairs but demonstrated difficulty with producing rhymes.	Model and scaffold in the areas of rhyme production.

Tables

Date: 11/15			
Objective: Multiplication Fact Fluency			
Name: Susan	Name: Donny	Name: Carlos	Name: Isabel
Name: Jason	Name: Jordan	Name: Marquis	Name: Kelly
Name: Anthony	Name: Ricardo	Name: Linh	Name: Jeremiah

Figure 3.1. Data Collection During Observations.

Table 3.4. Guiding Questions—Diagnostic

Source of Data	Guiding Questions to Consider
Diagnostic	• Does the assessment target specific areas of concern? • Do the results answer questions about ability, motivators, triggers for negative behavior, or areas of strength? • Do the results seem consistent with other assessment measures? • Are the data specific enough to create a statement to be used to design a plan of action?

Diagnostic Assessment in Behavior

A functional behavioral assessment (FBA) is a diagnostic evaluation technique used to determine the function of a student's behavior and the factors that maintain the behavior. In other words, observers need to determine why a student is behaving as observed and what is encouraging the behavior to continue or increase. It helps teachers and other educators understand the reason(s) for the student's behavior. They can then use this information to design an intervention to teach the student a new, more acceptable way of getting what he or she wants. The process of completing an FBA includes the following steps:

- Identify and define target behavior and replacement behavior
- Collect data
- Identify the function of the behavior (for example, attention, avoidance)
- Design an intervention
- Implement the intervention
- Evaluate the intervention

For numerous resources, refer to the Positive Behavioral Intervention and Supports (PBIS) Center at https://www.pbis.org/. The positive behavioral interventions and supports (PBIS) framework is an evidence-based, tiered framework for supporting students' behavioral, academic, social, emotional, and mental health goals and needs. When implemented with fidelity, PBIS practices, procedures, and strategies improve students' social-emotional competence, academic success, and school climate. The health and well-being of teachers and students is enhanced by a positive, predictable, equitable, and safe learning environment.

Summative Assessment

Summative assessments provide data related to a student's comprehensive learning after an established period of instruction. This can occur at the end of units of study, school year, and/or as required by state and/or district mandates. Usually, the purpose of mastery assessments and evaluation is related to decisions regarding programs for students to meet their instructional needs. These mastery, summative assessments provide a summary of learning by students in a class, program, or special services. As previously mentioned, numerous school districts use the results of summative state assessments aligned with the state curriculum standards to make decisions related to promotion and subsequent student programs. In addition, school districts and/or state departments of education use summative assessments for program determinations, school grading, and other evaluations to comply with educational policies. Administrative actions from mastery, summative assessments are often high stakes, with implications set in state and school district policy. It is imperative that teachers and other instructional personnel are knowledgeable about the high-stakes summative assessments that directly impact students. Student assessment data from these summative assessments can and should be used as part of the universal screening assessment data within unit and lesson planning processes.

This cycle of DDDM uses multiple sources of assessment, aligned with national and state curriculum standards and benchmarks, to meet the academic and behavioral needs of students through establishing effective classroom and behavioral expectations, developing effective unit and lesson planning, and providing high-quality instruction and interventions based upon multiple sources and types of assessment data within classrooms. Table 3.5 provides an overview of the four types of assessments and use by teachers and other school personnel.

> Stop and Reflect:
>
> What does it mean to say "assessment guides instruction"? What are some ways to make this happen? What are the benefits of using a variety of assessments? Any disadvantages? How do you fit assessment into your own classroom instructional time? Are any changes needed to make it more effective for you within the DDDM process?

ENSURING EQUITY IN ASSESSMENT

Despite the best efforts of many educators, some assessments can become more subjective than objective. Other assessments may be biased by privileging prior experiences over actual measuring of student learning or ability, putting students who may have had different prior experiences than the school culture at risk for performing

Table 3.5. Types of Assessments Used by Educators

	Universal Screening	Progress Monitoring	Diagnostic	Summative
Definition	Initial determination of broad base of student performance	Skill-based, ongoing, sensitive to small changes in student learning	In-depth, specific information about knowledge and skills	Final determination of broad base of student performance
Uses	Broad benchmark attainment index (initial)	Specific academic or behavioral target	Specific academic domain of knowledge, skills, or abilities	Broad benchmark attainment index (final)
Student Focus	School-wide	Class or small group	Individual student	School-wide
Frequency	Annually/three to four times per year	Every three weeks/weekly	Annually (or as needed) for in-depth evaluation	Annually
Instruction	Class/school curricular/program decisions	Effectiveness of instruction and interventions	Selecting appropriate programs and/or educational placements	Align with curriculum goals and instructional planning process
Implication	First step in instruction and intervention planning	Continue and/or revise instruction and/or interventions	Program or curriculum planning	High stakes, based on state and school district policies

more poorly on assessments. Educators should take great care to ensure that assessment is as nonbiased as possible. Ways to do this include considering multiple data sources, looking at all aspects that affect student learning (for example, classroom and home environment), and relying on more than simply grades to form judgments about student progress. Care should be taken to ensure that assessments are culturally sustaining and relevant to students from marginalized backgrounds. Gated screenings are an equitable approach, allowing educators to look at multiple data sources simultaneously (Klingbeil et al., 2019). The gated approach combines test scores from multiple assessments (for example, fall standardized test scores and spring math unit tests) to better understand student strengths and weaknesses than one type of measure alone (Van Norman et al., 2017). Consider measuring developmental progress and formative assessments regularly rather than relying on high-stakes and summative assessments as smaller improvements among struggling learners may be lost when looking at overall scores. Finally, educators should approach assessment as holistic, taking into account context and culture. Test scores alone do not paint a detailed picture of a student and are influenced by multiple factors, such as student culture (for example, language spoken, country of origin, prior experiences) and classroom culture (for example, teacher instructional strategies, match between home and school culture) that may affect student learning and behavior (Yee and Butler, 2020).

Practical Guidelines for Classroom Assessments

Classroom teachers and other school-based educators engage in the DDDM process on a daily basis using informal assessments including observations, work sample analyses, and initial curriculum-based assessments and measurements. The following section describes and provides examples of informal assessments.

Observations

Students should be observed while they are working on performance tasks, during instructional lessons, while working independently and in small groups, and during large group instruction. Observations can and should be completed throughout instruction as they provide initial and continuous information about student learning. Teachers observe students as they complete academic tasks to identify conceptual understandings, procedural accuracies, and misunderstandings of the content standards during instruction, as well as collect formative assessment data to make decisions about further instruction and/or interventions in academic areas.

Table 3.6. Guiding Questions—Observations

Source of Data	Guiding Questions to Consider
Observations	• Does the student appear interested and engaged in the learning? • How often does the student answer questions or need assistance? • Does the student use calculators, manipulatives, etc. often and accurately? • What are the areas of strength? • What are the areas of need? • Are the observations consistent or do they show a trend with other sources of assessment data?

> **Preparing for an observation:**
>
> What specific behaviors do you want to collect information about?
> What specific students will you be observing?
> How will you record the information as you observe?
> What will students be doing during the observation?

It is helpful to record observations in an organized manner. Charts and tables can be completed to organize the data collected during the observation, to review and to use with individual students, small groups, or other educators. Charts and tables can be efficient tools to note observations on student performance. Brief notations are recorded on student performance related to specific lesson objectives or curricular goals. See previous examples of data collection in figure 3.1.

Data collection through observations is also an objective form of measurement that enables teachers, instructional coaches, and/or behavior specialists to identify specific behavioral concerns, to set behavioral goals, and to collect continuous progress monitoring data to determine the effects of behavioral plans. Prior to data collection, educators should define the target behavior and the desired or replacement behavior in precise, observable terms for clear and accurate data collection.

There are several specific data collection strategies focused on behavior to use when observing students in classrooms. Table 3.7 provides the source/name of data collection strategy and definitions.

Table 3.7. Samples of Data Collection—Behavior

Data Collection Strategy	Definition and Guiding Questions to Consider
Frequency or Event Recording (see figure 3.2)	Measurement of the number of times a behavior occurs within a given period. • How often does the student show the identified behavior? • Does the behavior appear to be increasing or decreasing? • How does this behavior compare to others in the classroom? • Are the observations consistent or do they show a trend with other sources of assessment data?
Duration Recording (see figure 3.3)	Measurement of the length of time a student engages in a specified behavior. • How long does the behavior last? • As you observe, do you believe the student has the ability to complete the requested academic tasks? • What else do you observe in the classroom during this time?
Latency Recording (see figure 3.4)	Measurement of the length of time between when a direction is given and when the student initiates the requested action. • Did the student hear or focus on the direction? • As you observe, do you believe the student has the ability to complete the requested academic tasks? • What else do you observe in the classroom during this time?

Student: _____

Class/Teacher: _____ Observer: _____

Time/Length of Observation: _____

Behavior: _____

Instructions: Make a mark each time the behavior occurs. To calculate rate,[1] divide the total number of occurrences by the length of the observation.

Date	Time Started	Time Ended	Total Time	Tally	Total Occurrences	Rate
11/14	Ex.: 8:30 am	Ex.: 8:45 am	15 min.	//// //// //// ///	18	18/15 min. = 1.2/min.

1. If the observation periods are the same length, rate calculations might not be necessary.

Figure 3.2. Event Recording Form Example.

Student: _____ Date: _____

Class/Teacher: _____ Observer: _____

Time/Length of Observation: _____

Behavior: _____

Time Start	Time End	Duration
Example (digital stopwatch) 00:00	*04:27*	*4 minutes, 27 seconds*
Example (wall clock) 8:30	*08:57*	*7 minutes*
	TOTAL/AVERAGE	

Additional comments:

Figure 3.3. Duration Recording Form Example.

Time of Request of Cue (Actual Time)	Time Behavior Was Initiated	Latency (Time between Prompt and Compliance)

Figure 3.4. Latency Recording Form Example.

During the observation of student behavior within a classroom, several of the critical questions listed previously relate to the student's ability to complete the academic task as directed or requested by the teacher. Therefore analyses of work samples and assignments provide important, additional information during the data collection phase of DDDM.

Work Sample Analyses

A critical aspect of comprehensive assessment includes careful analysis of students' work products. These products can include performance tasks from in-class assignments, board work, and problem-based learning assignments.

Table 3.8. Guiding Questions—Work Samples

Source of Data	Guiding Questions to Consider
Work Sample Analyses	• Does the student follow the directions (oral or written) about the task? • Does the student accurately represent the information? • Does the student complete all sections of the task? Accurately? Independently? • Does the student use accurate skills when completing the task? • What are the areas of strength? • What are the areas of need? • Are the observations consistent? Do they show a trend with other sources of assessment data?

Work sample analyses can be a powerful source of data for teachers. Student work is tangible evidence of what students are able to do and provides a range of responses related to the different learning goals and tasks. Student work may include writing samples, student journals, homework assignments, reports, math performance tasks, and artwork. Two specific assessment techniques that evaluate student work are portfolios and rubrics. A portfolio is a data collection approach that involves collecting and analyzing a series of individual student work samples over a period of time. The samples are organized in a binder or notebook, which consists of completed student selected for assessment and/or evaluation purposes.

Rubrics are a set of scoring guidelines for evaluating students' work samples. The guidelines consist of scales that define levels of performance for specific tasks. Educators use rubrics to assess students' performance based on a set of standards that communicate high-quality, average, and low-quality work. Rubrics may include general or specific information depending on the purpose. General rubrics describe the criteria of successful work in general terms and can be applied to a variety of tasks or problems. Specific rubrics reflect the same criteria as general rubrics do, but they include much more detail about specific tasks rather than sets of tasks. Sharing rubrics with students before they are assessed so they are aware of the expectations is recommended.

Curriculum-Based Assessments (CBA)

CBAs are used to evaluate students' performance on particular levels of mastery in the curriculum. This form of evaluation identifies skills that students have mastered and those that need to be mastered. These assessments can be developed using the scope and sequence charts from the curriculum (as aligned with district and state standards and benchmarks). Some are also packaged and published on federal sites and commercially (see the following websites for more information).

CBM RESOURCES AND PROBES

easyCBM: http://easycbm.com
Intervention Central: www.interventioncentral.org
Center on MTSS: https://mtss4success.org/essential-components/progress-monitoring
National Center for Intensive Interventions-Diagnostic Tools: https://intensiveintervention.org/tools-charts/example-diagnostic-tools

---

Table 3.9. Guiding Questions—CBAs

Source of Data	Guiding Questions to Consider
CBAs	• Does the assessment align with state and district standards and benchmarks? • Does the curriculum have inventories available? • Were student results consistent with other assessments? • What are the areas of strength? • What are the areas of need? • How will I use this information when planning for instruction?

Curriculum-Based Measurement (CBM)

CBM is an effective and efficient means of assessing and monitoring students' ongoing progress in the curriculum. These formative assessment tools measure mastery of knowledge and skills of students and their learning progression in the core academic areas. Educational psychologist Stanley Deno (2003) began research on CBM in the mid-1970s. His research was evidence that commercially prepared tests that were "stand-alone" or that accompanied textbooks did not have reliable and valid mastery tests. A CBM system should (a) be easy to construct, (b) be quick to administer and score, (c) be usable by all, (d) have technical adequacy, and (e) allow time series data to be collected on student programs.

In short, CBM is a powerful assessment tool teachers can use to both test and measure student progress. CBM probes are typically given to students to assess their reading, spelling, writing, and mathematics skills. Educators who implement CBM briefly test students, usually once or twice a week, based on academic content from their school curriculum. These tests, or "probes," are intended to be brief, lasting anywhere from one to five minutes, depending on the skills they want to measure. For example, in mathematics, drawing directly from the mathematical skills and materials of the school curriculum, a teacher might give students eight questions and five minutes to complete them all. As another example, in reading, a teacher can give students a one-minute reading test. Upon completing the probe, the educator records the number of correct and incorrect answers or words.

According to Espin and colleagues (2017), the key components of CBM include the following:

- Define the specific skill to be assessed and timeframes for assessment administration.
- Provide a lesson/unit objective that is measurable.
- Include criteria for mastery.
- Develop administration directions to ensure uniformity.
- Create assessments by randomly selecting a set number of items.

The results of the CBM/CBA probes provide information of individual student learning progression within classrooms. The probes are scored on accuracy of performance, fluency and skill knowledge, and speed. These probes provide samplings of the knowledge and rate of learning to inform continuous DDDM regarding instruction. In essence, CBM guides classroom instruction (Powell et al., 2022). Based on an individual student's correct and incorrect responses, teaching practices can be continued or intensified. Decisions regarding instructional variables such as the instructional time (dosage), grouping arrangement (individual instruction instead of small group), or specific methods and/or resources can be made by the teacher and/or members of the MTSS team.

The results of the assessments from CBM/CBA measures are then recorded and graphed to visually display learning progress within a particular timeframe to clearly view students' learning progressions and trends over time (see figure 3.5.) Plotting these points against the expected performance in various subject areas helps school administrators, teachers, and parents visualize the student's academic progress.

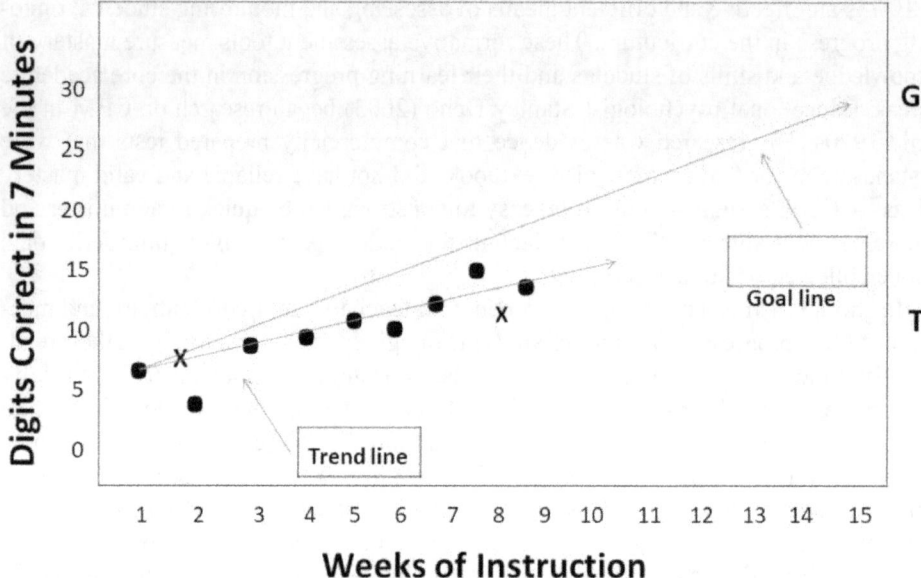

Figure 3.5. Sample of a Progress Monitoring Graph.

CBM was developed to be an efficient, valid, and reliable opportunity to monitor student growth and to inform instruction and interventions within the DDDM process and is necessary for action planning and decision-making by teachers in action research and/or members of the MTSS teams. This ongoing method is easily accessible for classroom application and implementation and is an analysis of student learning from instruction and interventions within classrooms (Espin et al., 2017).

> Stop and Reflect:
>
> What forms of assessment do you currently use? Of the assessments you currently use, what types are they? Why do you use them? How do the different types of assessment you currently use influence your instruction?

Using Assessment to Plan Instruction

Clearly student learning depends on two major factors. The first factor is the interactive connections among the unique characteristics and needs of students, the curricular goals and content, and instructional methods and resources. The second factor is effective identification and use of validated and evidence-based instructional practices and interventions to address student learning of the curriculum and exhibiting behavioral expectations based upon assessment data. Teachers who regularly collect assessment data about student performance gain valuable information to make subsequent decisions through DDDM. For any assessment data to have a positive impact on student learning, teachers and other school personnel need to collect, analyze, and interpret data to differentiate instruction, individualize plans, and intensify interventions. The important thing is to remember that this process is an ongoing cycle of curriculum, instruction, and assessment as informed by multiple, ongoing assessments.

The multiple sources of available assessment data provide the necessary feedback to teachers, parents, and students. Teachers, along with other school-based personnel, use the results from the assessment data during the DDDM process in action research to address the needs of students and/or to provide information to MTSS support team members, as needed. In addition, these data can be very motivating for students and can facilitate communication between teachers and parents (Gesel et al., 2021). Sometimes the DDDM process is completed by individual teachers; at other times, it is completed in collaboration with parents and other professionals on the grade-level and/or the school-wide MTSS team. Student performance will be improved if the process is informed by assessment data that are aligned with the curriculum benchmarks and the specific needs of the students.

As teachers use assessments to plan instruction and interventions for students in classrooms, multiple formative assessments provide consistent feedback about student learning (Austin and Filderman, 2020). These formative assessments are informal, with interactive, timely feedback and response. They are intended to monitor student learning and to inform teacher practice as a critical component of decision-making for adjustments to instruction and interventions to assure content mastery of curricular outcomes. Progress monitoring assessments capture the rate and growth of a student or students in response to the instruction. In some cases, diagnostic assessment information may also be used to specifically identify instructional misconceptions.

As mentioned at the outset of this chapter, teachers use various assessments for classroom decision-making within both the AR process and MTSS framework. Data collection and analyses of each type of assessment ensures that the subsequent decisions made through the DDDM process addresses individual students' academic and behavioral needs. Chapter 5 describes the process of DDDM related to the phases of action research by teachers and other school-based educators. In addition, teachers and other school-based personnel use, interpret, and act upon the results of various formative assessments to accurately determine and evaluate students' academic and behavioral needs within the MTSS framework in the schools. Chapter 4 describes the use of assessment results within the tiers of instruction and intervention in the MTSS framework. There may be times that additional resources, interventions, and/or personnel with specific expertise may be needed to address and/or intensify interventions for students with more high-intensity needs as determined by members of the MTSS team. In the next chapter, definitions, components, and benefits of the MTSS framework are described. Essential components of assessing effective instruction, curriculum enhancement, differentiated instructional practices, and intensifying interventions are related to assessment, instruction, and interventions within the three tiers of MTSS.

> **Stop and Reflect:**
>
> Consider how the assessments that you use provide information for the DDDM process in instruction. How do these assessments improve your DDDM in instruction and interventions? Do the results from the classroom assessments and DDDM in your classroom through your action research inform discussions and decisions by the members of the grade-level MTSS team at the school level?

As you continue to learn about, use, and increase your knowledge about various types and uses of assessments to inform the DDDM process by educators, there are so many opportunities. The following list includes many suggestions for next steps to increase your knowledge and improve your skills with the use of various assessments for developing academic and behavioral goals and interventions for students.

> **Additional actions that you might consider include:**
>
> Familiarize yourself with the types of assessment used within MTSS. Write down the currents assessment practices utilized within your classroom/school.
>
> If you do not already have a universal screening tool and/or progress monitoring resources in place in your school, visit the websites provided. Discuss with colleagues those that will benefit your students most effectively.
>
> If you already have those tools in place, evaluate the benefits of their use and determine their significance with your students.
>
> Review your instructional DDDM processes and identify how they align with your current benchmarks/standards.
>
> Identify which students may be identified as per the universal screening data. This identification will help guide you in planning for additional supports within the tiers.
>
> Determine how you purposefully use assessment practices in your classroom to evaluate your teaching practices.

SUMMARY

The use of various assessments during DDDM provides a continuous improvement model for teachers and other educators to integrate and focus instruction and interventions to specific instructional and behavioral needs of students. Various types of assessments focus instructional concerns of one student, groups of students, or students throughout the school. Specifically, guidelines for successful use and implementation of various forms of assessments include the following:

- Assessment data are the basis for planning in instruction and interventions.
- Confirm that multiple assessments are available and all educators are knowledgeable about use (for example, standardized assessments, district and school-mandated assessments, diagnostic and progress monitoring probes).
- Learn about each type of assessment for use by teachers to assure accurate use and interpretation of results.

Teachers use multiple sources of assessment data to plan to improve student learning and behavior. This information is the basis for us to continuously analyze, revise, and enhance instruction and determine academic and behavioral interventions within the DDDM process. There are four types of assessments that are important within DDDM in MTSS: universal screening, progress monitoring, diagnostic, and summative. Each type of assessment provides the basis for instructional planning integral to meeting the needs of all students within classrooms and schools.

Stop and Reflect:

In the vignette, Ms. Hernandez is observing some initial concerns for several of the students in her class. The use of multiple sources of data (for example, assessments, observations, reviews of student products, etc.) provides individual teachers and groups of teachers and other educators with information to identify an instructional concern, develop and implement an intervention plan, and collect and analyze results. Consider the students in your classroom and review various sources of data to identify an instructional concern. As you consider various assessments, review the websites provided to identify several assessments that Ms. Hernandez could use to learn more about her students' learning needs.

KEY TAKEAWAYS

There are four types of assessments that are important within DDDM in MTSS: universal screening, progress monitoring, diagnostic, and summative.

Multiple assessments within DDDM are integral to implementation of MTSS within schools and action research by teachers.

Assessment data are integral to the instructional planning process for academics and behavior.

Resources and supports to ensure equitable and quality implementation are necessary.

Where can I find information about assessments for data collection and analyses?

Resource	Description	Link
Diagnostic Tools (Reading, Math, Behavior)	Multiple resources and examples of diagnostic assessments through the National Center of Intensive Interventions.	https://intensiveintervention.org/tools-charts/example-diagnostic-tools
Multiple Assessments for Progress Monitoring	Multiple, researched resources and assessments to use within the MTSS framework, a source of the American Institutes of Research.	https://mtss4success.org/essential-components/progress-monitoring
Reviewed Assessment Tools in Multiple Content Areas	Multiple, researched resources and assessments to use within the MTSS framework, a source of the National Center for Intensive Interventions at the American Institutes of Research.	https://intensiveintervention.org/tools-charts/identifying-assessments

Resource	Description	Link
Resources for Assessments and Interventions Focused on Behavior and Social-Emotional Skill Development	Positive behavioral interventions and supports (PBIS) is an evidence-based, tiered framework for supporting students' behavioral, academic, social, emotional, and mental health. When implemented with fidelity, PBIS improves social emotional competence, academic success, and school climate. It also improves teacher health and well-being. It is a way to create positive, predictable, equitable, and safe learning environments.	https://www.pbis.org/

REFLECTION QUESTIONS

1. Describe the similarities and differences among the various types of assessments used by teachers.
2. Name and describe the four components of DDDM. Why is assessment critical to this process?
3. Name and describe the types of assessments and their uses within the MTSS framework.
4. What assessment resources are available to you and your colleagues to conduct DDDM on various teams? Review several of the resources available on the federal sites included in this chapter. What resources could you use in your classroom?
5. As you consider the various opportunities to use various types of assessments, what current opportunities could be used by you and your colleagues to begin and/or enhance the expert use of assessments to plan instruction for your students?

REFERENCES

Austin, C. R., and Filderman, M. J. (2020). Selecting and designing measurements to track the reading progress of students with disabilities. *Intervention in School and Clinic, 56*(1), 13–21.

Consortium on Reading Excellence. (2008). *Assessing reading: Multiple measures for all educators working to improve reading achievement.* Novato, VA: Arena Press.

Deno, S. L. (2003). Developments in curriculum-based measurement. *Remedial and Special Education, 37*(3), 184–92.

Deno, S. L., and Fuchs, L. S. (1987). Developing curriculum-based measurement systems for data-based special education problem solving. *Focus on Exceptional Children, 19*(8), 1–16.

Diagnostic Data. (n.d.). Retrieved from https://intensiveintervention.org/intensive-intervention/diagnostic-data.

Espin, C. A., Wayman, M. M., Deno, S. L., McMaster, K. L., and Rooij, M. (2017). Data-based decision-making: Developing a method for capturing teachers' understanding of CBM graphs. *Learning Disabilities Research & Practice, 32*(1), 8–21.

Gesel, S. A., LeJeune, L. M., Chow, J. C., Sinclair, A. C., and Lemons, C. J. (2021). A meta-analysis of the impact of professional development on teachers' knowledge, skill, and self-efficacy in data-based decision-making. *Journal of Learning Disabilities, 54*(4), 269–83.

Gesel, S. A., and Lemons, C. J. (2020). Comparing schedules of progress monitoring using curriculum-based measurement in reading: A replication study. *Exceptional Children, 87*(1), 92–112.

Honig, B., Diamond, L., and Gutlohn, L. (2018). *The core reading sourcebook.* Oakland, CA: Arena Press.

Mason, E. N., and Smith, R. A. (2020). Tracking intervention dosage to inform instructional decision making. *Intervention in School and Clinic, 56*(2), 92–98.

Klingbeil, D. A., Van Norman, E. R., Nelson, P. M., and Birr, C. (2019). Interval likelihood ratios: Applications for gated screening in schools. *Journal of School Psychology, 76*, 107–123. https://doi.org/10.1016/j.jsp.2019.07.016

Kress, J. E., and Fry, E. (2016). *The reading teacher's book of lists.* San Francisco, CA: Jossey-Bass.

Lemons, C. J., Sinclair, A. C., Gesel, S., Gruner Gandhi, A., and Danielson, L. (2017). Supporting implementation of data-based individualization: Lessons learned from NCII's first five years. National Center on Intensive Intervention.

National Center on Intensive Intervention. (n.d.) Diagnostic Data. Retrieved from https://intensiveintervention.org/intensive-intervention/diagnostic-data

National Council of Teachers of Mathematics. (2020). *Principles and standards for school mathematics.* Retrieved from: https://www.nctm.org/uploadedFiles/Standards_and_Positions/PSSM_≠wlineExecutiveSummary.pdf

Powell, S. R., Bos, S. E., King, S. G., Ketterlin-Geller, L., and Lembke, E. S. (2022). Using the data-based individualization framework in math intervention. *Teaching Exceptional Children*, 00400599221111114.

Van Norman, E. R., Nelson, P. M., and Klingbeil, D. A. (2017). Single measure and gated screening approaches for identifying students at-risk for academic problems: Implications for sensitivity and specificity. *School Psychology Quarterly, 32*(3), 405–13. https://doi.org/10.1037/spq0000177

Yee, N., and Butler, D. (2020). Decolonizing possibilities in special education services. *Canadian Journal of Education, 43*(4), 1071–103.

Chapter Four

Multi-Tiered System of Supports

INTRODUCTION

Multi-tiered system of supports (MTSS) is an equity-focused framework designed to provide all students with high-quality, evidence-based instruction and intervention that is responsive to their strengths and needs. This chapter (a) details the essential components of the MTSS including the problem-solving approach, data-driven decision-making (DDDM), and evidence-based practices (EBP); (b) discusses how MTSS supports students to develop their academic, behavior, and social-emotional skills; and (c) introduces how action research (AR) fits within an MTSS framework.

OBJECTIVES

After reading this chapter, readers will be able to

- identify and define the essential components of the MTSS framework;
- explain the three tiers MTSS and how tiered instruction is responsive to student strengths and needs;
- explain how MTSS supports students in academics, behavior, and social-emotional development; and
- determine and evaluate how action research fits within the MTSS framework.

KEY TERMS

High-intensity needs: Students with high-intensity needs have significant and persistent needs that require intensive and sustained intervention (Slanda and Little, 2022).

Individualized Education Program (IEP): An IEP is a written legal document outlining the programs of special education instruction, supports, and services a child will receive to make progress in school.

Positive behavioral intervention and supports (PBIS): According to the Center on Positive Behavioral Interventions and Supports, PBIS is "an evidence-based three-tiered framework to improve and integrate all of the data, systems and practices affecting student outcomes every day" (n.d.).

Response to intervention (RtI): RtI is a targeted approach to identify students who are struggling academically and provide support to those who need it.

VIGNETTE

I met with several of my colleagues on our first-grade team to share concerns regarding student engagement and learning in my classroom. Several of them suggested whole-group engagement activities. As I tried them with my students, I observed that students who understood the lesson content had engaged with the activities. I observed that some of the students, especially those I was most concerned about, still did not engage in the lesson activities. I realized that I need to consider different strategies and activities for different groups of students and individuals.

Our school and district leaders are focused on DDDM, using student data to differentiate instruction and implement interventions within an MTSS framework. I have heard much about evidence-based core instruction, differentiated instructional practices, tiers, interventions, and progress monitoring. The goal is to reflect on our current teaching methods in our classrooms related to the learning by all our students. There have been several workshops and sessions within our grade-level professional learning community on the MTSS framework. I want to address the instructional needs for all my students. How do I begin?

—Ms. Hernandez

MULTI-TIERED SYSTEMS OF SUPPORTS

An MTSS is required by federal legislation, such as the Individuals with Disabilities Education Act (1997, 2004) and the Every Student Succeeds Act (2015) and supported by research (for example, Hoover et al., 2008; Lemons et al., 2018). Providing sufficient and effective instruction and intervention for all students is critical but can be challenging. Students who do not receive instruction that provides access to the core curriculum experience lower academic performance, higher dropout rates, negative behavioral and social outcomes, and limited prospects for higher education (Jackson, 2021).

However, MTSS is a comprehensive approach that strongly emphasizes equity and strives to improve educational opportunities and results for every student. MTSS presents an opportunity for schools and districts to integrate fundamental practices to address educational equity and support the academic, behavioral, and social-emotional learning (SEL) of all students through data-driven decision-making and evidence-based tiered supports (Jackson, 2021).

All students must be provided with access to the core curriculum. The amount of support students require will differ based on their individual strengths and needs. MTSS is a comprehensive framework that includes varying tiers of support to meet the individual needs of students. MTSS is a proactive and systematic approach for providing a continuum of evidence-based practices to immediately respond to students needs by leveraging their strengths through data-driven decision-making (Slanda and Little, 2020).

The MTSS framework is a three-tiered (or four-tiered, in some states) problem-solving framework that utilizes EBPs to deliver instruction and intervention. MTSS is a general education initiative (Batsche, 2014; Stoiber, 2014) designed to prevent learning failure through a proactive approach. For students who may struggle, MTSS addresses their needs through an intensifying intervention structure (Miciak and Fletcher, 2018). MTSS includes (a) EBPs at all tiers, (b) DDDM, (c) individualized and targeted interventions, and (d) progress monitoring (Lemons et al., 2017). MTSS matches high-quality instructional practices and curricular resources and materials to students' strengths and needs academically, behaviorally, and socially (Leonard et al., 2019). Figure 4.1 illustrates how MTSS is an equitable framework that provides academic, behavior, and SEL supports.

According to the CEEDAR Center, essential components include (a) high-quality, differentiated classroom instruction for all students; (b) systemic and sustainable change; (c) an integrated data system; and (d) positive behavioral support. Additionally, critical features of MTSS include (a) universal screening, (b) data-based decision-making and problem solving, (c) continuous progress monitoring, (d) a focus on successful outcomes, and (e) a continuum of evidence-based interventions (CEEDAR Center).

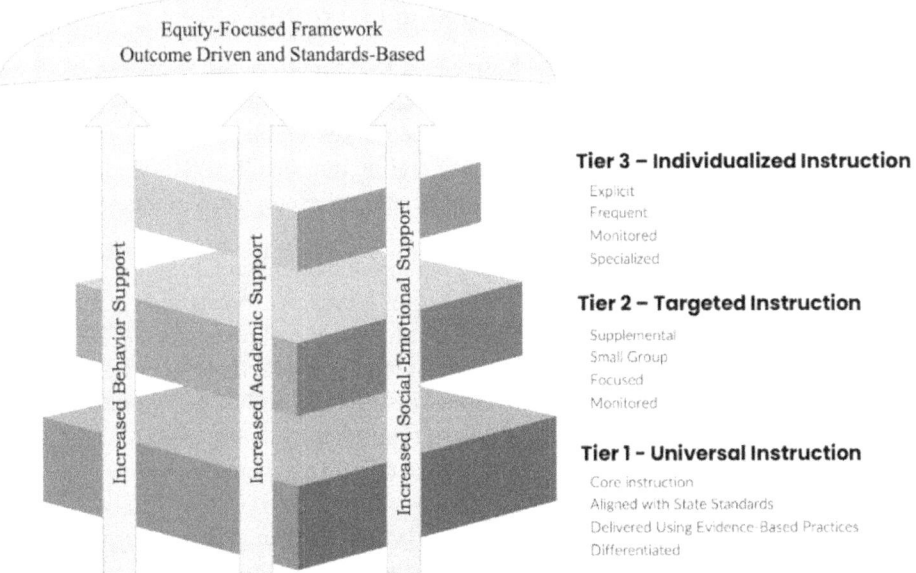

Figure 4.1. An Equity-Focused Framework of MTSS that Provides Academic, Behavior, and Social-Emotional Learning Supports. Adapted from Slanda et al., in press.

Table 4.1. Main Components of the MTSS Framework. Adapted from Slanda et al., in press.

MTSS Framework Main Components
• Supports all students in the general education setting • Problem-solving approach • Utilizes DDDM • Comprises a continuum of evidence-based instruction and intervention • Develops students' academic, behavior, and social-emotional domains • Designed to be flexible and fluid • Administers increasingly intensified instruction and intervention at each tier

Response to Intervention (RtI)

Response to intervention is a multi-tiered approach to providing instruction and intervention address students' academic needs. RtI is a targeted approach for providing high-quality instruction and universal screening to allow educators to identify and support students who may need additional instruction or intervention. Through progress monitoring and data analysis, educators predict, prevent, and remediate academic outcomes with increasing levels of instructional intensity. RtI is characterized by cultural and linguistic responsiveness, continuous assessment including universal screening and progress monitoring, and evidence-based intervention. According to the National Center on Intensive Interventions, RtI consists of four essential components: (a) universal screening, (b) EBPs and instruction, (c) progress monitoring, and (d) tiered instruction.

Positive Behavioral Intervention and Supports (PBIS)

According to the Center on Positive Behavioral Interventions and Supports, PBIS has been adopted by over twenty-five thousand schools. Similar to RtI, which supports students' academic growth, PBIS is an evidence-based and tiered framework to support students' behavioral, academic, social, and mental health. PBIS is an equitable and responsive approach to create an equitable and safe school environment where all students have an opportunity to succeed.

Within a tiered framework, preventative and proactive universal supports are delivered school-wide during tier 1. This tier enables educators to establish a foundation where the majority (80 to 85 percent) of students will experience success. During tier 2, a small number of students receive supplemental supports that target their specific needs. These supports can include additional instruction, additional opportunities for positive reinforcement, increased prompts or reminders, and increased adult support. For students who need intensive intervention, tier 3 provides individualized, comprehensive, and function-based supports.

Effective PBIS systems prioritize equity, center student outcomes, utilize data, emphasize evidence-based and equitable behavior practices, and invest in systems that support fidelity of implementation (Center on Positive Behavioral Interventions and Supports, 2022). The emphasis is on positive behavior strategies that prevent (not punish) inappropriate behaviors. PBIS has been linked to improved behavior and academic outcomes (Freeman et al., 2016; Kittleman et al., 2019).

Social-Emotional Learning (SEL) Supports

Incorporating SEL supports into MTSS provides a strong foundation for addressing the diverse needs of students (Lane, 2007; McCart and Choi, 2020). Students who have faced trauma experience gaps in their social emotional learning (Richard Albrecht and Brunner, 2019). Embedding SEL within MTSS can help address the gaps through a tiered, proactive, and positive approach. Additionally, embedding SEL within MTSS framework allows educators to reconsider how to address behaviors that may be the result of trauma. Addressing SEL through this equity-focused approach, also addresses students' academic and behavior needs (Albrecht and Brunner, 2019). Similar to PBIS, tier 1 of SEL is preventative and proactive. This tier includes school-wide adoption of SEL intervention strategies as well as opportunities for professional learning for teachers to enhance their knowledge of EBPs to support SEL instruction (Kim et al., 2019; Steed and Shapland, 2019). At tiers 2 and 3, educators can implement targeted and sustained SEL interventions for students who require individualized support. When SEL is embedded within MTSS frameworks, culturally responsive practices can be intentionally addressed (Steed and Shapland, 2019).

THE TIERS OF THE MTSS FRAMEWORK

Tier 1

READ MORE ABOUT IT!

Learn more about MTSS at https://mtss4success.org/.

Tier 1 includes the total student population. Tier 1 is core classroom instruction and should meet the needs of the majority of students (80 to 85 percent). Effective tier 1 instruction requires educators to assess whether they have created a positive and responsive learning environment that enables students to learn. Educators must also consider the accessibility and effectiveness of the curriculum and whether the curriculum meets classroom demands and individual student needs. Additionally, educators must reflect on whether they are employing responsive instructional strategies aligned with student learning needs (Slanda et al., 2022). Within tier 1, all students receive high-quality instruction delivered by the general education teacher (Howley et al., 2023; Leach et al., 2016). Typically, progress monitoring occurs three times a year, in the fall, winter, and spring, to assess student progress toward grade-level standards.

Teachers could ask the following questions about tier 1 instruction:

1. Is the evidence-based core instruction well delivered and effective?
2. Is the instructional coach available to provide feedback?
3. Are lessons aligned with grade-level standards?
4. What percent of students are achieving standards/benchmarks?
5. Which students are not achieving grade-level standards and why?
6. What assessment tools or processes were used to identify instructional needs and students' response to instruction?

Tier 2

Students who do not make sufficient progress in tier 1 are identified for tier 2 supports. During tier 2, students receive additional support through intensified interventions. These interventions supplement (not replace) tier 1 (Murawski and Hughes, 2009; Witzel and Clarke, 2015). Tier 2 includes increased instructional time (for example, an additional twenty minutes), smaller group sizes (for example, three to five students), and can include collaboration between general and special educators (Slanda et al., in press). Students receive additional opportunities to practice learning with increased guidance. Progress monitoring occurs at more frequent intervals, and there is intentional reinforcement of knowledge and skills (Fuchs and Fuchs, 2007; Harn et al., 2015).

At tier 2, teachers use assessment data to identify where and why tier 1 instruction was ineffective. This ensures educators do not replicate the same ineffective strategies or resources from tier 1 during tier 2 interventions. The strategies and resources in tier 2 should be aligned to meet the individual needs of students. It is also recommended that educators prioritize evidence-based and research-validated processes, strategies, and practices over the use of prepackaged intervention programs and products (Buffum et al., 2011; Hattie, 2008). Oftentimes, the prepackaged programs or products do not align with specific skill deficits and therefore do not meet the individual needs of students.

Teachers could ask the following questions about tier 2 intervention:

1. What targeted interventions were provided to improve outcomes for students who had not yet mastered academic, behavior, or social-emotional skills?
2. What changes to the environment, strategies, delivery, curriculum, or content can be made to enhance learning, behavior, or social-emotional support?
3. How effective was supplemental instruction for small groups of students struggling with academic, behavior, or social-emotional skills?
4. What was the frequency and duration of the intervention?
5. Were intervention(s) implemented with fidelity?
6. What progress monitoring assessments were used for data collection?

Tier 3

Tier 3 is the strongest level of intervention. During tier 3, students receive individualized one-on-one instruction tailored to their specific needs (Arden and Benz, 2018). Progress monitoring is more frequent, and educators may systematically implement multiple interventions simultaneously to determine the most effective approach for each student (Deno, 2015). Interventions during this tier 3 interventions are highly individualized and targeted, occur more frequently, and are longer in duration. The intervention is specialized and explicit. Like tier 2, tier 3 instruction supports and does not replace core instruction (tier 1). To determine the effectiveness of tier 3 interventions, educators may collaborate with other school personnel and parents, and they may engage in conversations about the data. Although the emphasis should be on providing intervention, it is equally important to collect sufficient data to determine a student's response to instruction and intervention.

Tier 3 interventions becomes a collaborative process that may include the general and special education teachers, instructional coaches, interventionists, behavior specialists, and others. Coaches, interventionists, and special education teachers may provide the specialized, intensive interventions directly or in consultation with the classroom teacher. The expertise that each professional brings to the team ensures students receive targeted interventions. In addition, the assessment data collected at each tier of instruction and intervention are important for the determination of a possible disability (Slanda and Little, 2018).

Students who do not respond positively to tier 3 interventions may be evaluated for special education services. The data collected during the tiered support is critical for making instructional decisions and determining eligibility for special education services. Students who receive intensive instruction tailored to their specific strengths and needs can make significant progress. However, when a student does not respond to tiered interventions, it may be due to a disability. This determination will ensure the student continues to receive individualized support and specially designed instruction as part of their special education services. Additionally, the use of DDDM (discussed in chapter 5) within the process of action research is an essential component for developing, implementing, and evaluating a student's individualized education program (IEP). By delivering special education services within the MTSS framework, students with disabilities are provided with meaningful access to the general education curriculum.

Teachers could ask the following questions about tier 3 interventions:

1. What targeted and individualized interventions and/or services were provided to improve outcomes for students who had not yet mastered academic, behavior, or social emotional skills?
2. What changes to the environment, strategies, delivery, curriculum, or content can be made to enhance learning, behavior, or social-emotional supports?
3. How effective is supplemental instruction for small groups of students struggling with academic, behavior, or social-emotional skills?
4. What was the frequency and duration of the intervention?
5. Were intervention(s) implemented with fidelity?
6. What progress monitoring assessments were used for data collection?
7. What does the team feel are appropriate next steps to support the student?

Centering Equity in MTSS

The MTSS framework strives to address well-documented educational disparities. By integrating a systematic set of procedures for screening, intervening, and monitoring students who demonstrate deficits before making evaluation decisions for disability placement, the framework is designed to reduce inappropriate referrals to special education. At the heart of equitable action research is a classroom in which daily instruction is equitable and of high quality. Culturally sustaining supports that consider the diverse needs of all learners should be an ongoing component of general class instruction and at the foundation of MTSS. Within equitable MTSS frameworks, universal screeners and progress monitoring assessments are conducted by trained and knowledgeable educators who collect data from multiple sources to identify learning difficulties across contexts, including home and school. Educators can also seek to identify strengths or assets across home environments as well, such as multilingualism, familial values, and diverse perspectives on educational issues. Importantly, educators must use evidence-based assessment instruments that are reliable and include diverse forms for monitoring student progress; they must avoid discriminatory practices against culturally and linguistically diverse students when administering assessments and provide assessments in the student's primary language (Linan-Thompson et al., 2022).

Equity-based MTSS is a school-wide, structural framework that uses data-driven decisions to ensure that all students receive academic, behavioral, and social emotional supports (McCart and Miller, 2020). In such a framework, typically marginalized students are at the center of the instructional process, and educators learn *from* their students rather than simply *about* their students. Students' various and complex intersecting identities are considered across all educational decisions with a goal of increasing academic and behavioral outcomes of students from CLD backgrounds, including those with disabilities. Consideration of the whole child, including socioemotional supports, is of the utmost importance as this may be necessary to mitigate years of educational inequities and discrepancies.

Cramer and colleagues (2023) established a framework for equitable MTSS that considers culturally sustaining procedures and examples of EBPs that align with academic and socioemotional supports across tiers of instruction. These procedures include (a) at tier 1, school-wide screening and culturally responsive education and socioemotional supports are provided for all learners; (b) at tier 2, culturally responsive targeted interventions that are individualized or small group based, culturally adapted and affirming, and involve feedback from diverse stakeholders; and (c) at tier 3, individualized assessments and cultural adaptations of evidence-based interventions based on individual student need and in consultation with stakeholders such as families and school-based mental health professionals as necessary.

ACTION RESEARCH WITHIN MTSS

Chapter 1 explains that action research is a method of testing and describing theories in which teachers analyze student learning in relation to classroom instruction (Yendol-Hoppey and Fichtman, 2020). This approach to teacher learning necessitates knowledge of data collection, evidence-based instructional practices and resources, and multiple types of assessments. With this knowledge, teachers can systematically reflect on their teaching and adjust their instruction based on careful analysis of their students' current classroom performance (Efron and Ravid, 2020). The goal is to enhance student learning as teachers continue to teach, implement new methods and resources, and reflect on the outcomes.

Conducting applied action research has been described as empowering for teachers by providing them with opportunities to develop within their professional roles and responsibilities (Gesel et al., 2021; Yendol-Hoppey and Fichtman, 2020). The data collection process within action research is so continuous and fluid. Daily, teachers gather data using both formal and informal assessment methods, which they then use to select evidence-based instructional strategies and resources. This knowledge enables teachers to make informed decisions and implement changes in the classroom, allowing for adjustments to be made to support student needs (Yendol-Hoppey and Fichtman, 2020).

The AR process includes four key phases that are integral throughout the implementation of each of the tiers within MTSS (see figure 4.2):

1. Identify the Problem
2. Develop and Implement a Solution
3. Collect and Analyze Data
4. Reflect and Share the Results

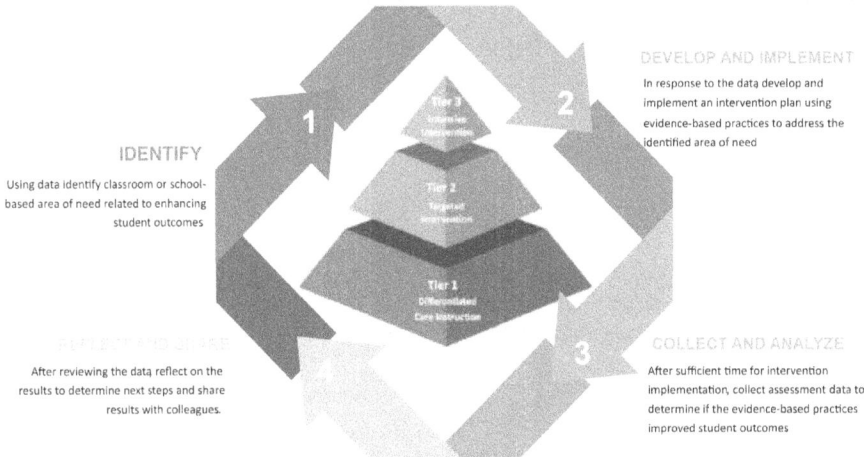

Figure 4.2. The Action Research Cycle.

Educators utilize both formal and informal assessments in their classrooms, and they have access to assessment results at the district and state levels. Action research does not involve conducting more assessments. Rather, it involves carefully examining the outcomes of current assessments and reflecting on whether the instructional methods led to improved student learning aligned with rigorous grade-level standards (Efron and Ravid, 2020). In addition to data collected from formal assessments, teachers analyze data from observations of student behavior or other informal measures. All data sources provide valuable information about academic, behavior, and SEL, enabling teachers to enhance their practices.

Collaboration with other professionals enhances the effectiveness of action research. When teachers and specialized instructional support personnel such as speech-language pathologists, occupational therapists, counselors, behavior therapists, and school psychologists collaborate, they share ideas, approaches, and data interpretations. Collaboration is particularly important when the initial solutions generated through action research fail to address the instructional concerns. As students progress through the tiers, educators come together to review and interpret assessment data. The data-focused conversations foster a deeper understanding of student learning needs.

To effectively meet complex student needs, teachers and other school-based educators prioritize and utilize data. The action research process within the MTSS framework promotes collaboration with a team of educators who investigate educational concerns and coconstruct solutions. The action research process is an important part of MTSS meetings, during which current assessment data is reviewed, hypotheses are developed, and the effectiveness of specific instructional methods and interventions are investigated.

MTSS teams should address the following questions:
- What do students need to know and be able to do?
- What will we do to ensure learning?
- How will we know when they have met standard/benchmarks?
- What additional supports may be needed?

Stop and Reflect:

Ms. Hernandez is concerned about the learning of several of her students. After reviewing this initial information about the tiers of instruction and intervention within the MTSS framework, what questions should she consider? What would be some next steps for her to take?

During discussions among teachers and school-based educators within MTSS meetings, it is critical to develop an action plan based upon the assessment data during all the tiers of instruction and interventions. Table 4.2 contains critical elements to record and consider by the members of the MTSS team.

Table 4.2. Determining Student Supports

School:	Classroom Teacher:	Grade Level/Subject Area:
MTSS Team Members:		Date:

Providing Supports	
What is the grade-level standard of performance?	
What is the student's current level of performance?	What assessments were used to determine performance level?
What is the targeted benchmark, and what intervention can assist the student in achieving the benchmark?	
What are the student's strengths?	What are the student's areas for support?
What are the instructional expectations/goals for the student related to the identified problem?	
What is the gap between expected level of performance and the actual current level of student performance?	

SUMMARY

MTSS provides a framework for educators to address student strengths and needs related to academics, behavior, and social-emotional well-being. MTSS involves collaboration of educators with various expertise who engage in the action research process. Within the MTSS framework, teams of educators gather and analyze data to design and implement instruction and interventions. High-quality instruction grounded in EBPs are prioritized. Instruction is individualized and intensified using both student strengths and needs as a guide. This process involves utilizing multiple sources of assessment data to determine, implement, and evaluate specific action plans tailored to meet student needs.

Throughout this process, it is crucial to prioritize high-quality instruction that is grounded in EBPs. In addition, it is important to consider and utilize additional resources, collaborative expertise, interventions, and scaffolded support within the classroom. These elements should be implemented through ongoing systems of support at each tier within the MTSS framework. Chapter 5 will present specifics of how educators can execute DDDM as part of the action research process and the MTSS framework.

KEY TAKEAWAYS

MTSS is an equity-centered framework for delivering instruction and intervention to students to support their academic, behavior, and social-emotional learning.

A three-tiered MTSS framework includes essential components such as universal screening, DDDM, problem-solving approach, ongoing progress monitoring, emphasis on positive student outcomes, and a range of evidence-based interventions.

The MTSS framework encompasses the action research process, which involves teachers continually monitoring student progress by gathering and analyzing data, devising hypotheses, implementing instruction and intervention, and reflecting and collaborating.

Where can I find more information about MTSS?

Resource	Description	Link
Center on Multi-Tiered Systems of Supports	Center on MTSS provides technical assistance, resources, and tools to support states and districts in the implementation of MTSS.	https://mtss4success.org/
National Center on Intensive Interventions	NCII provides technical assistance, resources, toolkits, training, and implementation supports to states, districts, and educator preparation programs to implement MTSS and intervention.	https://intensiveintervention.org
Branching Minds	Branching Minds provides resources, support, and products related to MTSS, PBIS, and SEL to support districts and schools.	https://www.branchingminds.com/mtss-guide

Resource	Description	Link
I-MTSS	I-MTSS is an integrated MTSS model of support that brings together a research network that includes the Meadows Center, Ci3T, IMFR, and IMTSS at UCONN. Each of these projects includes resources to assist educators.	https://mtss.org
Center on PBIS	Center on PBIS shares tools, publications, resources, and presentations/videos to support schools and other agencies.	https://www.pbis.org/
RTI Action Network	RTI Action Network is a program from the National Center for Learning Disabilities and provides information related to RtI.	http://www.rtinetwork.org/

REFLECTION QUESTIONS

1. Provide an overview of MTSS, highlighting its key components.
2. Explain RtI, PBIS, and SEL and how they fit within the MTSS framework.
3. Describe the distinguishing features of each tier within the MTSS framework.
4. Consider how action research fits within the MTSS framework. Explain how you can apply your knowledge of action research and MTSS to improve student outcomes.

REFERENCES

Arden, S. V., and Benz, S. (2018). The science of RTI implementation: The how and what of building multi-tiered systems of support. *Perspectives on Language and Literacy, 44*(4), 21–25.

Balu, R., Zhu, P., Doolittle, F., Schiller, E., Jenkins, J., Gersten, R., and Jacobson, J. (2015). Evaluation of response to intervention practices for elementary school reading: Executive Summary. US Department of Education, Institute of Education Sciences, National Center for Education Evaluation and Regional Assistance.

Batsche, G. (2014). Multi-tiered system of supports for inclusive schools. Handbook of effective inclusive schools: Research and practice, 183–196.

Buffum, A., Mattos, M., and Weber, C. (2011). *Simplifying response to intervention: Four essential guiding principles*. Solution Tree Press.

CEEDAR Center (2023). Multi-Tiered system of supports chapter. https://ceedar.education.ufl.edu/mtssudldi-professional-development-module/mtss-chapter/#MTSS%20Components

Center on Positive Behavioral Interventions and Supports (2022). What is PBIS. https://www.pbis.org/

Cook, B. G., and Cook, S. C. (2013). Unraveling evidence-based practices in special education. *The Journal of Special Education, 47*(2), 71–82.

Council for Exceptional Children and CEEDAR Center (2017). High-leverage practices. Council for Exceptional Children and CEEDAR Center. https://ceedar.education.ufl.edu/wp-content/uploads/2017/07/CEC-HLP-Web.pdf

Deno, S. L. (2015). Data-based decision-making. In *Handbook of response to intervention: The science and practice of multi-tiered systems of support* (pp. 9–28). Springer US.

Efron, R., and Ravid, R. (2020). *Action research in education: A practical guide.* Guilford.

Every Student Succeeds Act, Public Law 114-95, 114th Cong., 1st sess. (2015).

Freeman, J., Simonsen, B., McCoach, D. B., Sugai, G., Lombardi, A., and Horner, R. (2016). Relationship between school-wide positive behavior interventions and supports and academic, attendance, and behavior outcomes in high schools. *Journal of Positive Behavior Interventions, 18*(1), 41–51.

Fuchs, L. S., and Fuchs, D. (2007). A model for implementing responsiveness to intervention. *Teaching Exceptional Children, 39*(5), 14–20.

Gesel, S. A., LeJeune, L. M., Chow, J. C., Sinclair, A. C., and Lemons, C. J. (2021). A meta-analysis of the impact of professional development on teachers' knowledge, skill, and self-efficacy in data-based decision-making. *Journal of Learning Disabilities, 54*(4), 269–83. https://doi.org/10.1177/0022219420970196

Harn, B., Basaraba, D., Chard, D., and Fritz, R. (2015). The impact of schoolwide prevention efforts: Lessons learned from implementing independent academic and behavior support systems. *Learning Disabilities: A Contemporary Journal, 13*(1), 3–20.

Hattie, John (2008). *Visible learning: A synthesis of over 800 meta-analyses relating to achievement.* Routledge.

Hoover, J. J., and Soltero-González, L. (2018). Educator preparation for developing culturally and linguistically responsive MTSS in rural community elementary schools. *Teacher Education and Special Education, 41*(3), 188–202.

Howley, A., Allan, D. M., Howley, N. L., and Furst, T. (2023). All means all . . . maybe: MTSS policy and practice across states in the United States. *Mid-Western Educational Researcher, 35*(1).

Individuals with Disabilities Education Act.

Jackson, D. (2021). *Leveraging MTSS to ensure equitable outcomes.* American Institutes of Research.

Kim, E. K., Anthony, C. J., and Chafouleas, S. M. (2022). Social, emotional, and behavioral assessment within tiered decision-making frameworks: Advancing research through reflections on the past decade. *School Psychology Review, 51*(1), 1–5.

Kittelman, A., McIntosh, K., and Hoselton, R. (2019). Adoption of PBIS within school districts. *Journal of School Psychology, 76*, 159–67.

Lane, K. L. (2007). Identifying and supporting students at risk for emotional and behavioral disorders within multi-level models: Data driven approaches to conducting secondary interventions with an academic emphasis. *Education and Treatment of Children, 30*(4), 135–64. https://doi.org/10.1353/etc.2007.0026

Leach, D., and Helf, S. (2016). Revisiting the regular education initiative: Multi-tiered systems of support can strengthen the connection between general and special education. *Journal of the American Academy of Special Education Professionals, 116,* 124.

Lemons, C. J., Sinclair, A. C., Gesel, S., Gruner Gandhi, A., and Danielson, L. (2017). *Supporting implementation of data-based individualization: Lessons learned from NCII's first five years.* National Center on Intensive Intervention.

Lemons, C. J., Vaughn, S., Wexler, J., Kearns, D. M., and Sinclair, A. C. (2018). Envisioning an improved continuum of special education services for students with learning disabilities: Considering intervention intensity. *Learning Disabilities Research & Practice, 33*(3), 131–43.

Leonard, K. M., Coyne, M. D., Oldham, A. C., Burns, D., and Gillis, M. B. (2019). Implementing MTSS in beginning reading: tools and systems to support schools and teachers. *Learning Disabilities Research & Practice, 34*(2), 110–17.

McCart, A. B., and Choi, J. H. (2020). State-wide social and emotional learning embedded within equity-based MTSS: Impact on student academic outcomes. Research Brief. SWIFT Education Center.

Miciak, J., and Fletcher, J. M. (2020). The critical role of instructional response for identifying dyslexia and other learning disabilities. *Journal of Learning Disabilities, 53*(5), 343–53.

Morin, A. (n.d.). What is response to intervention (RTI)? Understood.org https://www.understood.org/en/articles/understanding-response-to-intervention

Murawski, W. W., and Hughes, C. E. (2009). Response to intervention, collaboration, and co-teaching: A logical combination for successful systemic change. *Preventing School Failure, 53*(4), 267–77.

Office of Special Education Programs. (2021). Individuals with Disabilities Education Act (IDEA) database. US Department of Education. https://www2.ed.gov/programs/osepidea/618-data/state-level-data- files/index.html#bcc

Richard Albrecht, N. M., and Brunner, M. (2019). How positive behavioral supports and social-emotional curriculum impact student learning. *The European Journal of Social & Behavioural Sciences*.

Slanda, D. D., and Little, M. E. (2018). Exceptional education is special. In *The Wiley handbook of teaching and learning*, 277.

Slanda, D. D., and Little, M. E. (2020). Enhancing teacher preparation for inclusive programming. *SRATE Journal, 29*(2), n2.

Slanda, D. D., and Little, M. E. (2022). Developing special educators to work within tiered frameworks. In *New considerations and best practices for training special education teachers* (pp. 115–36). IGI Global.

Slanda, D. D., Pike, L. M., Herbert, L., Wells, E. B., and Pelt, C. (2022). Dismantling disproportionality in special education through antiracist practices. In *Equity in the classroom: Essays on curricular and pedagogical approaches to empowering all students*, 218.

Slanda, D. D., Pike, L. M., and Little, M. (In press). *The general educator's guide to inclusive education: Essential knowledge, skills, & dispositions*. Rowman & Littlefield.

Steed, E. A., and Shapland, D. (2020). Adapting social emotional multi-tiered systems of supports for kindergarten classrooms. *Early Childhood Education Journal, 48*, 135–46.

Stoiber, K. C. (2014). A comprehensive framework for multi-tiered systems of support in school psychology. In *Best practices in school psychology: Data-based and collaborative decision making*, 41–70.

Witzel, B., and Clarke, B. (2015). Focus on inclusive education: Benefits of using a multi-tiered system of supports to improve inclusive practices. *Childhood Education, 91*(3), 215–19.

Yendol-Hoppey, D., and Fichtman, N. (2020). *The reflective educator's guide to classroom research: Learning to teach and teaching to learn through practitioner inquiry*. Corwin.

Chapter Five

Data-Driven Decision-Making

INTRODUCTION

This chapter calls for teachers, instructional coaches, and other classroom and school-based educators to consider why data-driven decision-making (DDDM) and action research (AR) within classrooms and schools are integral to meeting the instructional, behavioral, and social-emotional needs of students with diverse learning needs. Consistent with federal legislation (for example, the Every Student a Success Act, 2015), educators work within a multi-tiered system of supports (MTSS) framework for data collection, analysis, and intervention. This chapter provides educators with descriptions of the phases, resources, and tools necessary to complete DDDM within the MTSS framework. In addition, this chapter connects DDDM with action research.

OBJECTIVES

After reading this chapter, the reader will be able to

- describe DDDM within the MTSS process,
- discuss the phases of the DDDM process,
- describe various resources to use during the phases of DDDM, and
- connect the DDDM process with the AR process.

KEY TERMS

Fidelity of implementation: The delivery of instruction in the precise way in which it was designed.
Pedagogical practices: The theory and practice of teaching. Pedagogy refers to the methodology and process for how instructors approach teaching and learning using a specific curriculum with specific goals in mind.
Triangulation: The process of collecting multiple sources of data for the problem (phenomenon) or issue being studied.

VIGNETTE

Ms. Hernandez has continued concerns regarding the learning of all of the students in her first-grade class. Educators at her school administer weekly mini assessments as progress monitoring probes for the students that are aligned with the district and state curriculum standards. She is most concerned that all of her students are not mastering the standards. Several of her colleagues on the first-grade team also described similar concerns. Earlier in the week, the entire team attended professional development about DDDM, as this is a priority in the school and district. Her team decided to try to implement the DDDM with the support of their literacy and mathematics coaches. The members of the team reviewed the information shared previously about the MTSS framework and action research, including the resources that could be used within their school. They also identified time for data chats once per week. Ms. Hernandez was going to focus on reading, and one of her colleagues was going to focus on mathematics. They brought the materials from the professional development and specific school and classroom assessment results to their next meeting. The goal of the meeting was to discuss specific instructional concerns of students through a DDDM process to develop an implementation plan with Ms. Hernandez to address the identified concerns.

MAKING IT HAPPEN: IMPLEMENTING DDDM

Meeting the learning needs of all students in a class can be a daunting task, especially given diverse learning needs. With so many demands on teachers' time, even finding time to learn about the students and their backgrounds, skills, and abilities can be difficult. However, the essential question for each teacher must be: "Are all of my students learning?" In order to accurately answer this question, it is critical to continuously observe, think about, and analyze student learning to ensure mastery of grade-level curricular standards and expectations. The DDDM process provides specific procedures for educators to become more efficient and effective. This is because specific instructional needs based on student data are identified. When instructional decisions are made based on classroom data, instruction and interventions are purposely designed and aligned to target the specific identified strengths and needs of students. This process of analysis and reflection provides the information needed to identify classroom instructional concerns, develop and implement instruction and/or intervention plans, and collect and analyze data for continued actions after reflection. In addition, the four phases of the DDDM process invariably spiral through the tiers of the MTSS framework. As described in the previous chapter on MTSS, DDDM occurs within and throughout each of the tiers of instruction and intervention to address the instructional concerns of students within the classroom, small groups, or individual students in need of increasingly intensive interventions and dosage.

This chapter is purposefully written to outline and describe the phases of the DDDM process to clearly depict the interrelationship of each phase of the cyclical and continuous DDDM process that is used within each of the tiers of the MTSS framework (Slanda and Little, 2018). The process of DDDM is used by teachers and/or groups of educators throughout the tiers at grade level team, content team, and/or MTSS meetings. The focus of DDDM for specific students may vary throughout the tiers, but the four phases in the DDDM process remain the same as shown in the external cycle of figure 5.1.

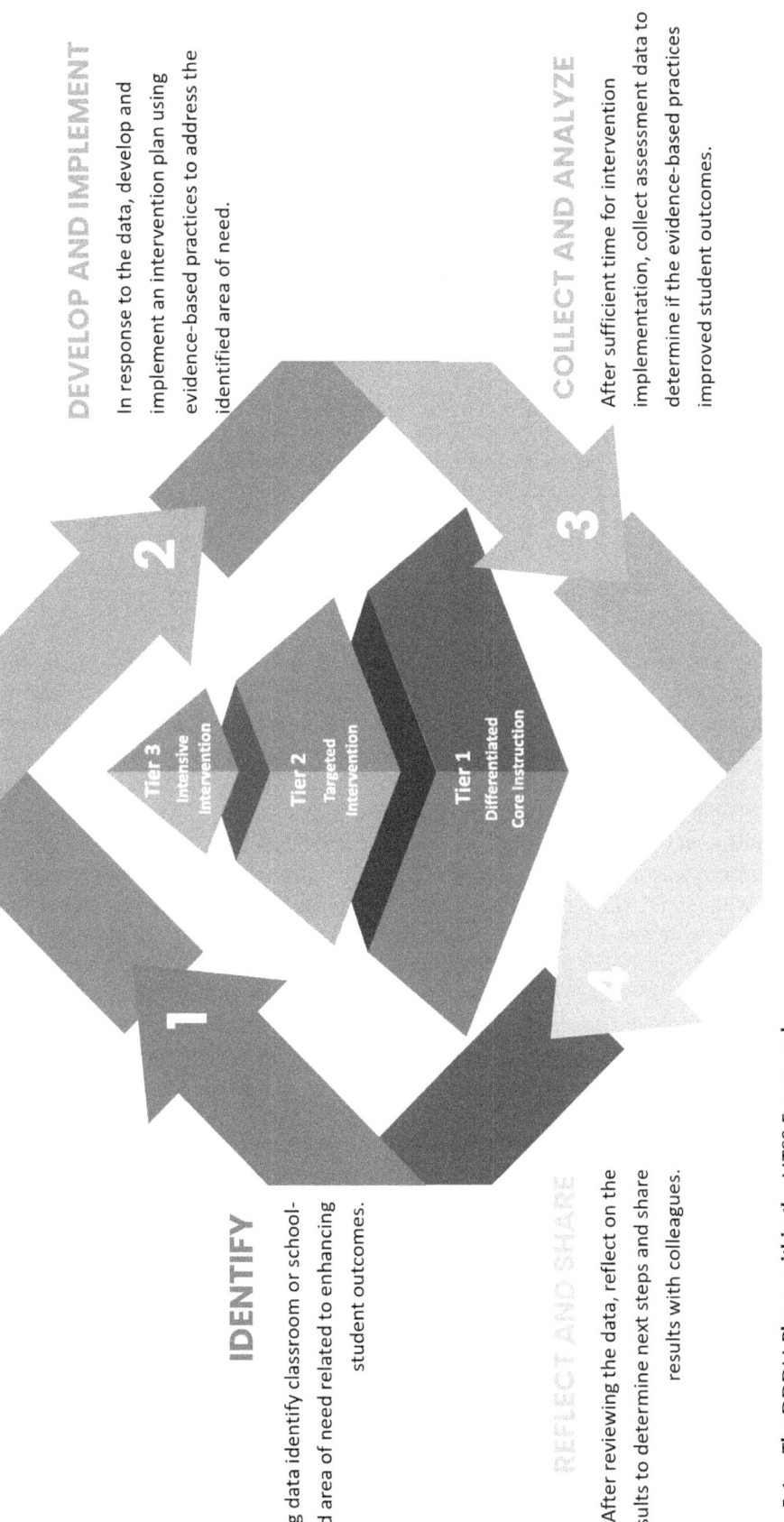

Figure 5.1. The DDDM Phases within the MTSS Framework.

Therefore the four phases of the DDDM process drive the development of instructional and intervention plans for identified students, both small groups and individual students, based upon collection and analyses of various sources of assessment data within each of the tiers of the MTSS framework. To articulate and illustrate the phases of the DDDM process within the MTSS framework, the vignette of Ms. Hernandez will be described to illustrate and provide examples and templates within each of the phases.

> Stop and Reflect:
>
> Ms. Hernandez and the teachers on the grade-level team discussed the three tiers of the MTSS framework. How would you describe each of the tiers? How would this process be different or the same within each of the tiers? Think about and share what questions and/ or resources might be required. (Review the information in previous chapters, if needed.)

THE PHASES OF THE DDDM PROCESS

Teaching, as a profession, is similar to medicine. Before doctors treat a patient, they must first learn as much as possible about the concerns, identifying the source of the problem areas to address and the questions to be answered or phenomenon to be explained. At times, doctors must review previous records, meet with and interview the patient and family members, and prescribe additional diagnostic assessments. They often collaborate with other health and medical professionals to accurately diagnose the problem and prescribe appropriate medical treatments for the patient.

Classroom teachers, instructional coaches, and other school personnel who are involved with the DDDM process within the MTSS framework must begin the process by identifying an issue in the classroom that is an area of concern during tier 1. The focus on tier 1 instruction is student learning from differentiated, core instruction. For example, what need is reflected when the level of student learning does not meet grade-level classroom academic or behavioral expectations? To adequately identify a classroom problem during tier 1 instruction, a teacher must take the time needed to investigate the initial areas of concern by collecting and analyzing information specifically aligned to the student's learning needs related to the grade-level curriculum expectations. Teachers who rush to complete the problem formulation stage are more likely to flounder in their later efforts, whereas teachers who take their time to reflect on and define their problem are more likely to pursue questions yielding meaningful results (Sagor and Williams, 2016). As mentioned earlier, this process can be completed individually, in teams, or collaboratively within the school.

Phase 1: Identifying an Area of Need

To begin the DDDM process within the MTSS framework, teachers must first observe, question, and reflect on the entire classroom, a group of students, or an individual student in order to investigate a concern. They evaluate the current situation and compare it to the expectations and curricular standards for all of the students. This additional, specific data helps to identify the classroom problem or issue to study. At the begin-

IDENTIFY NEED

Using data, teachers and other educators identify classroom areas of need related to enhancing student academic or behavioral outcomes.

ning of this process, it is important to consider curricular standards or behavioral expectations as they determine goals for the students. Then teachers review current information about the students in the class. Informal assessments can be used to collect additional behavioral or academic information while observing or interacting with the students to determine specific instructional strengths and concerns. This process may take time. Teachers observe and interview students while engaged in learning, analyze their work samples, and collect classroom assessments. It can also be helpful to collaborate with another teacher, mentor, or instructional coach at this point—especially a knowledgeable colleague who has observed the students in the class. These informal observations and assessments can be used to collect initial or ongoing performance or achievement information. For example, if the instructional goal for the students in first grade is to understand the nature of language, specific, observable data could be collected by the teacher using specific criteria. See the example in figure 5.2.

As the classroom teacher is observing, collecting informal assessment information, and reflecting on the strengths and concerns of the students in the class, several considerations and questions support this reflective process. To assist teachers with the process of identifying an area of need for a student or a group of students, there are probing questions to guide the initial phase, which involves observation, reflection, and analysis of student work. Data collection and careful consideration of these questions will help with the identification a specific classroom problem.

During this phase, not only is it important to consider the students' characteristics and learning in relation to the current curricular standards and behavioral expectations, but it is also important for teachers to reflect on the current instructional approaches and techniques used in the classroom. Teachers use multiple instructional resources and pedagogical practices in a classroom. As mentioned in earlier chapters, curricular content, behavioral expectations, and instructional practices have an impact

Strand: LANGUAGE – K-12		
LA.D.1 Understands the nature of language		
LA.D.2 Understands the power of language		
Criteria	Yes	No
1. Uses language appropriate to situation/listener		
2. Understands word meanings		
3. Uses words effectively to get needs met		
4. Uses a variety of vocabulary words when talking		
5. Has trouble thinking (finding) the right word to say		
6. Has trouble saying what he/she is thinking		
7. Describes things to people		
8. Sequences events in the correct order*		
9. Uses correct grammar when talking*		
10. Uses complete sentences when talking*		
11. Expands on an answer or provides details*		
12. Explains what he/she has heard*		

Figure 5.2. Curricular Observation Informal Assessment: Language.

Table 5.1. Considerations When Identifying Needs

Questions to consider when identifying a need:

1. *What concerns do I currently have regarding the students in my classroom?*
2. *In order to investigate my concerns, what information and/or assessment data do I need?*
3. *Where will I find this assessment data? How will I collect assessment data?*
4. *What academic goals or behavioral expectations should my students master?*
5. *To address the identified needs of my students, what goals should be set?*
6. *What are some practices and resources that align with the identified goals?*

on student learning and achievement. Current, evidence-based practices (for example, direct instruction, peer tutoring, computer-assisted instruction) must be clearly identified by the teacher. Often these instructional variables are some of the least intrusive to change and positively impact student achievement.

After reflecting on current concerns and addressing the questions, teachers identify several different instructional concerns to target for the identified needs of specific students. They focus on a problem that is a priority learning need, which when addressed can produce positive results for the students. Additionally, it is critical that the chosen need is aligned with the curricular standards for students as determined within the grade level, school, district, and state.

After consideration of these multiple variables during this phase of DDDM, the teacher develops a problem statement. This statement becomes the basis for DDDM and the resulting action plan for instruction and intervention. It provides not only a description of the problem but also the goal for improvement related to the problem. Adequately identifying a classroom problem helps with setting appropriate goals for students, which can result in accelerated learning.

Once a classroom problem has been identified, the problem statement is developed. It should be a clear, concrete, specific description of the problem answering the four questions. The first phase of classroom instructional DDDM process focuses instruction and leads to a more effective and efficient way to teach because it is specifically targeted on student learning based on current assessment data. The next phase of the classroom instructional DDDM process focuses on developing and implementing an action plan that includes choosing an instructional focus, data collection strategies, and an implementation schedule.

> The problem statement needs to answer these four questions:
>
> Who is affected by the problem?
> What might be causing the problem?
> What is the goal for improvement?
> What might be done about the problem?

The problem identification phase can be completed individually, collaboratively, or in conjunction with the members of the grade level or MTSS team within the school. As with each of the phases of this very important process, classroom teachers will initially begin with their current instructional concerns. In this particular example, Ms. Hernandez is completing this process with her colleagues at the first-grade level meeting. During any phase, the individual or team of teachers may request assistance from either other educators within the school or members of the MTSS team. Refer to table 5.2 and table 5.3. The next phase of the classroom instructional DDDM process focuses on developing and implementing an action plan that includes choosing an instructional focus, data collection strategies, and an implementation schedule.

Table 5.2. Example of Problem Statement

Sample: Identifying a Classroom Problem
Name(s): *Ms. Hernandez*
School: *ABC Elementary School*
Grade Level: *First Grade, Language Arts*
Problem Statement: Compose a problem statement specifically describing <u>who is affected</u>, <u>supported causes of the problem</u>, the <u>goal for improvement</u>, and <u>what might be done about the problem</u> as stated. (Provide as much specific information as possible.)
One of our first-grade students with specific learning disabilities and language impairments is having difficulty learning to read and write. He entered first grade reading instructionally at the preprimer level and consistently scoring a level 1 on the writing rubrics. After further investigation, we found that the student has poor letter/sound correspondence, weak phonemic awareness and phonics, and a limited repertoire of sight words. Our goal for the student is to build the letter sound correspondence while improving his ability to hear and record sounds in words. In addition to the regular reading and writing instruction, he will receive small group instruction geared to meeting his goal for improvement.

Table 5.3. Template of Problem Statement

Identifying a Classroom Problem
Name(s):
School:
Grade Level:
Problem Statement: Compose a problem statement specifically describing who is affected, supported causes of the problem, the goal for improvement, and what might be done about the problem as stated. (Provide as much specific information as possible.)

Stop and Reflect:

Think about the diverse academic and behavioral needs of students. What various sources of information and assessment data are available to specifically identify specific concerns? As you consider your teaching practices, what are various pedagogical practices that you could use within a classroom to address diverse learning needs of students?

Phase 2: Develop and Implement

This phase of the DDDM process focuses on the development of the specific instructional or intervention plan to address the needs and concerns identified from data review and reflection. The plan is a blueprint or actions for immediate change with instruction or more intensive intervention for the identified student(s) in the classroom. Before writing the specifics of the instructional or intervention plan, it is helpful to outline actions by answering the "what?" the "how?" and the "when?" This section names and describes the specific components to consider when completing plans to meet the identified needs of the students, as aligned with curricular expectations, during phase 2 of the DDDM process.

There are three important and interrelated instructional components during this phase of DDDM: evidence-based instruction, high-quality classroom implementation with fidelity, and continuous progress monitoring. These three instructional components are critical to the development and implementation of an instructional or intervention plan for improved student achievement. Teachers should collect multiple sources of assessment data related to the teaching and learning process within their classrooms. They must also consider how the resources and instructional materials used and the fidelity of their implementation impact student outcomes as determined through continuous monitoring of learning progress. All three components are equally important in each of the three tiers of the MTSS framework.

Evidence-Based Practices (EBP)

> **LEARN MORE ABOUT IT**
>
> High-impact researched EBP by John Hattie, titled *Visible Learning*: https://visible-learning.org/.

There is a vast array of instructional resources, materials, and interventions that claim to improve student learning outcomes. More than ever, educators are expected to make instructional decisions that use methods and programs that have been researched to improve student learning outcomes. From policymakers to classroom teachers, educators need ways to separate misinformation from research and to distinguish scientific research from poorly supported claims. Identifying the research validation processes used in instructional resource development ensures that educators understand and use the most effective instructional resources and interventions, based on scientific evidence. Components used to review the research on educational practices and programs include the following:

- Employ systematic, empirical methods that draw on observations or experiment.
- Involve rigorous data analyses that are adequate to test the stated hypotheses and justify general conclusions.
- Rely on measurements or observational methods that provide valid data across evaluators and observers, and across multiple measurements and observations.
- Select resources accepted by a peer-reviewed journal or approved by a panel of independent experts through a comparatively rigorous, objective, and scientific review.

High-Fidelity Implementation

Fidelity of implementation is the delivery of instruction in the precise way in which it was designed. In other words, instructional resources, methods, and practices must be used by teachers in their classrooms as designed and as implemented in the research that demonstrated improved student learning. Although both common sense and research support the concept of fidelity of implementation to ensure an intervention's successful outcome, the practical challenges associated with achieving high levels of fidelity are clear. These factors are related to complexity, resources required, teacher perceptions, and teacher skills. Specific proactive practices that help to ensure fidelity of implementation include the following:

- Link interventions to improved student outcomes.
- Specifically describe techniques, methods, and components.
- Clearly define the responsibilities of specific persons.
- Create a data system for measuring operations, techniques, and components.
- Create a system for feedback and decision-making (formative) based upon data from continuous progress monitoring.

Continuous Progress Monitoring

Within the MTSS framework, ongoing progress monitoring is used to determine whether students are responding to the developed and implemented plan from the DDDM process. Within the DDDM process, data collected from multiple sources must be identified to ensure that student results will be monitored in any of the tiers of the MTSS framework. Typically, in tier 1, students are screened to determine specific concerns by the classroom teacher, as described in the previous chapter. Once academic or behavioral goals are identified, developed, and implemented to address concerns, progress is monitored periodically to determine whether students are improving. If data show little to no change over a relatively brief period of time (for example, four to six weeks), students may be recommended for additional intervention through the DDDM process and may proceed to a more intensive tier. Student performance over time illustrates whether the student is achieving appropriately, that is, responding well to the instructional practices or interventions delivered.

> **READ MORE ABOUT IT**
>
> For examples and numerous resources of Progress Monitoring probes, review the National Center on Intensive Interventions at https://intensiveintervention.org/tools-charts/overview
>
> and
>
> the National Center on Student Progress Monitoring at https://files.eric.ed.gov/fulltext/ED502450.pdf.

Two primary methods for monitoring progress involve the use of measures for academic skills and/or behaviors that are closely associated with student outcomes (that is, robust indicators) or actual tasks in goal-level material (that is, curriculum sampling). For example, a robust indicator in reading could be one-minute samples of oral reading fluency. For a behavior goal, observations may include the collection of data on the frequency of the desired behavior. In a curriculum sampling approach, student progress could be determined by monitoring performance on samples of items that represent the most critical curricular skills to be mastered by the end of the year. A variety of methods can be used successfully to gauge student progress over time in a particular subject area. Additional information about progress monitoring can be found at the National Center on Intensive Interventions at https://intensiveintervention.org/tools-charts/overview, the Center on Positive Behavior Intervention Supports at https://www.pbis.org/, and the National Center on Student Progress Monitoring at http://www.studentprogress.org. Also, please refer to the chapter on assessments for additional information.

> Stop and Reflect:
>
> As you consider the information shared in the vignette of Ms. Hernandez, take a few moments to reflect on the following important questions in the DDDM process: Why are evidenced-based instructional practices and continuous progress monitoring important? What are three guiding principles for implementing a classroom instructional DDDM plan? If you were a member of the school's MTSS team, what would you suggest as part of the DDDM plan for the students in her classroom? (HINT: Remember to review chapter 3 of this book for additional information and multiple resources of assessments.)

Phase 3: Collect and Analyze Data

Educators use numerous classroom-based, formative assessments to provide feedback related to ongoing student learning. Therefore teachers select, use, and analyze assessments that provide information related to the specific classroom questions. In this section of the chapter, questions and checklists are provided to assist readers in identifying the data collection strategies (classroom assessments) that are related to the specific instructional need identified in the previous phases. In addition, various data collection sources for monitoring student learning related to the instructional or intervention plan will be described. This section of the chapter provides a brief overview of assessments for data collection and connects with the third phase of the DDDM process. Refer to chapter 3 for detailed descriptions and specific, additional examples of assessments for data collection.

Curriculum, Instruction, and Assessment

Curriculum, instruction, and assessment are integral and interrelated components of teaching and learning. Teachers must be knowledgeable about curriculum standards and able to articulate classroom expectations in relation to those standards and the individual needs of the students in the classroom. These curriculum standards establish the content to be learned by the students in the class. The instructional focus is the instructional practices and materials used by the teacher to teach curricular expectations. Assessment provides the data needed to answer the critical question: "Are my students learning and meeting the curricular goals and behavioral expectations?" Teachers use the evidence collected from assessments from the continuous progress monitoring pro-

Table 5.4. Reflective Questions—Focus

Reflective questions to address include:
1. *Based on my evidence, do I continue implementing the instructional focus?* 2. *Should I modify my instructional focus to better meet the needs of my students?* 3. *If the practice is not having an impact, should I study and implement another approach?*

cess to make decisions. The information received through data collection guides the classroom instructional DDDM processes through the tiers of the MTSS framework.

Data Collection with Various Assessments

In order to build a complete picture of student learning and behavior, assessment data from many sources are gathered to understand student learning and to measure the impact of classroom instruction within academics. In addition, assessments (for example, observations, interviews) provide important data to develop intervention plans that address classroom expectations and behavior. Using only one form of assessment can be misleading because it is a snapshot of an individual's ability on the particular day and time when assessed. Gathering evidence from many different sources over a period of time provides a broader and deeper understanding of student knowledge, learning, and behavior. In research terminology, the process of collecting multiple sources of data for every problem (phenomenon) or issue being studied is called triangulation. Triangulating data may seem time consuming and overwhelming at first, but it is efficient and effective because students' specific needs are explicitly and clearly defined during the DDDM process (for example, preassessment, continuous progress monitoring, and summary).

Meaningful DDDM should be a part of classroom teachers' daily work, not something extra for them to do. Hence, selecting the data collection strategies to use simply means thinking about life in the classroom/school and the ways that life can be naturally captured as data (Yendol-Hoppey and Fichtman, 2020). Within the instructional process, educators are continuously gathering and using data from their classrooms throughout the day. Direct assessments are clearly defined in specific, operational terms within a checklist of task analysis components to develop and implement plans to address behavior. Teachers and other educators observe the teaching, intervention, and/or student behavior to determine the percentage of occurrence, accuracy, or severity. Checklists used in observations, curriculum-based informal tests, and progress monitoring standardized measures are examples of direct assessment measures.

> Stop and Reflect:
>
> As you consider various types of assessments, consider your current classroom and school, and reflect upon the assessments that may be available for your use in the DDDM process. Questions to reflect upon include: Do the assessment instruments and methods selected measure the described outcome? Are the assessment instruments and methods selected easy to administer and score consistently? How is continuous progress monitoring completed in a consistent and reliable way? Have multiple sources of classroom data and assessments been identified and made available? What types of assessments should Ms. Hernandez consider?

Assessment and data collection are important throughout the process of DDDM. Collecting and analyzing assessment data during screening, prescribing additional assessments to further diagnose the presenting instructional concerns, monitoring the instructional progress, or summarizing the outcomes for a specific period of time (for example, length of intervention, grading period, annual progress) are used by teachers and other educators daily. By asking questions, collecting data, intervening, and continuously monitoring student progress, teachers, like doctors, prescribe instruction and interventions to meet the instructional and behavioral needs of all students. Because of the multiple types of assessments, the various uses of assessment data, and the importance of interpretation of the results from multiple assessments, teachers need increased expertise in each of these areas.

> **LEARN MORE ABOUT IT!**
>
> Check out the assessment tool charts at the National Center on Intensive Interventions at https://intensiveintervention.org/tools-charts/overview.

Phase 4: Reflect and Share Professional Learning

To align and maximize the DDDM process within the MTSS framework, purposeful, sustained professional learning to reflect and share student assessment data is needed (Yendol-Hoppey and Fichtman, 2020). Coordination and communication among each of the educational partners provides valuable input for continuous improvement (Gesel et al., 2021). Once data have been collected and reviewed by the teacher, the members of the grade level, and/or the MTSS team, plans for the next steps based upon those data are needed. If the results show improvement and mastery of the academic and/or behavioral goals, the team can decide to continue the instruction and intervention plans as developed. However, if the results do not evidence improvements, the DDDM process would need to be initiated again to identify the concerns more specifically and adjust or intensify the initial DDDM plan. This process may require additional professional learning, support, and resources to more intensively and accurately address the academic and/or behavioral issues. In this way, the cyclical nature of the DDDM process through each of the tiers is also a source of continuous learning for educators.

Continuous learning ensures high-quality implementation of the DDDM process by educators within schools. There are multiple, collaborative professional development structures that provide opportunities for educators to engage in discussions and learning about DDDM and evidence-based resources to improve student learning. Data team meetings, professional learning communities, lesson studies, and portfolios have been instituted as sources of continued learning among educators within schools. Through ongoing professional learning and collaboration with colleagues, knowledge and skills to improve, use, and enhance DDDM with fidelity occurs. The final chapter in this book describes professional learning opportunities and resources in more detail.

The use of assessment data to inform instruction occurs continuously in schools through team meetings, data chats, and school improvement team meetings to reflect on and refine teaching practices to address student needs (Little, 2012). During these meetings, assessment data are analyzed and various instructional and intervention methods, programs, and procedures are discussed and planned to address individual and/or groups of students' needs. By collecting additional assessment data after instruction, analyzing the results, and reflecting on subsequent plans, additional adjustments to instruction, including possible interventions and resources from other sources (for example, interventionists, special education teachers), may be needed to meet the instructional needs of identified students. This process may be repeated until student achievement is improved and the learning goals are achieved. If students (individuals or small groups) continue to experience difficulty mastering the instructional goal(s) and curricular standards for the grade level, increased and focused strategies, accommodations, and/or various intervention programs are planned and implemented within the classroom. The next chapter describes more fully the continuous process of DDDM within the tiers of the MTSS process with the profession and educational field.

> **REFLECT AND SHARE**
>
> After reviewing the data, reflect on the results to determine next steps and share with colleagues.

DDDM WITHIN THE AR PROCESS

At the outset of this book, the definitions and components of action research and traditional research were described and compared. Specifically, action research is defined as a process in which teachers systematically reflect on their practice and make changes to their instruction based on careful analysis of current assessment data of their students. Unlike traditional research in which researchers study the teachers, action research is conducted by classroom teachers with the goal of improving student learning within their classrooms. During action research, the teacher becomes the primary researcher. As researchers, teachers are key to analyzing instructional concerns and individual student issues within their classrooms. Although specific purposes, resources, assessments, and methods of analyses may vary, the critical process within action research and traditional research is DDDM. Similarly, the DDDM process is integral to the MTSS framework and similar to the goal, process, and analyses used by teachers in the action research process. During the final section of this chapter, the DDDM phases and resources will be illuminated with the vignette of Ms. Hernandez and specific examples and templates specifically related to and enhanced as the AR process.

Given that the DDDM process is initiated by teachers and may occur in any of the three tiers of the MTSS framework, the process and decisions made within each of the phases are made by the teachers, either by themselves or in collaboration with knowledgeable educators. The resulting plan is referred to as either an instructional or intervention plan, depending on the content and intensity of the plan. When developing a plan, teachers and members of the grade-level or school-wide MTSS team should reflect on, study, and answer a series of questions that focus their planning to address the identified student needs.

There are specific questions to consider when completing DDDM within action research.

Table 5.5. Reflective Questions in DDDM Process

DDDM Step	Questions to Consider
Pose a research question	What student learning will be studied? What evidence-based instructional practices will be studied?
Define learner outcomes	What specific student learning will occur related to the grade-level curriculum standards and goals?
Develop an instructional focus	What evidence-based instructional practices will I implement that will focus on the classroom problem or issue to be changed? How will I ensure fidelity of classroom implementation?
Identify data collection sources	What evidence do I need to collect? How will I collect the data? How often will I collect data? Are the data sources aligned with the instructional focus and learner outcomes? How will I ensure continuous progress monitoring?
Determine a level of support	What support do I need from my colleagues? Who will assist me with fidelity of implementation?
Outline an implementation schedule	How will I implement this plan? What is my timeline? When will I report back with the MTSS team on student results?

Pose a Research Question

As described in the first chapter, teachers and instructionally focused educators are critical to addressing issues of learning for all students. Similar to medical doctors, educators must collect, interpret, develop, and implement an action plan based upon data. This DDDM process is integral to action research. From the discussions and reflections on the information presented, teachers must develop a research question individually or in collaboration with other instructional personnel. This carefully formed question will be addressed by the implementation of the instructional or intervention plan. The research question must be even more specific than the problem statement and should focus on a measurable change or improvement. An effective research question must have four specific characteristics.

Identify a desired change in student learning. When composing a research question, specify the area of learning to improve or change. Avoid focusing on improving test scores as the desired change. For example, "How can teaching research-based metacognitive strategies in content classes improve scores on state-administered assessments?" State-administered assessments could be used as one data source (for example, a source to measure student learning). However, it should not be considered as a desired change in student learning. An example focusing on student learning may include, "How will modeling and providing practice in evidence-based metacognitive strategies effect my students' abilities to monitor their comprehension when reading?"

Be specific and measurable. The research question should be specific to student learning and the instructional practice that will be implemented. A research question guides the process, so specificity is important. In addition, specificity also supports improved fidelity of implementation.

Be answerable in a reasonable amount of time. It's important to pose a research question that can be studied and answered in a reasonable amount of time. Remember to choose a topic of study that is relevant and attainable. Consider both curricular standards as units of study and progress monitoring assessments when considering "reasonableness" of time.

Cannot be answered with a "yes" or "no" response. When wording a research question, try to avoid using words that answer the final question with a "yes" or "no." Begin a question with words such as "how," "when," or "why." An example may include, "How can modeling through read-alouds improve students' abilities to organize, analyze, synthesize, and interpret what they read?"

Tables 5.2 and 5.3 have an example of a problem statement and a template to use to complete this important process.

Define Learner Outcomes

When writing the instruction or intervention plan, think about the goals for student learning. After implementing the plan with fidelity, what improvement in achievement is expected for each of the students? Establishing high expectations and ambitious goals is important; however, the goals or outcomes must be attainable within a reasonable amount of time.

Develop an Instructional Focus

The evidence-based instructional practice(s) and/or intervention programs that the teacher chooses to implement and monitor with a specific group of students or an individual student is called the instructional focus. Finding a particular instructional focus may take time based on current knowledge, available resources, and teaching experiences of the teacher to address with the identified classroom problem. During this phase of DDDM, educators research methods and resources, study professional literature, attend professional development, engage in study groups and coaching, and consult knowledgeable support professionals within the school or district to continuously build upon their knowledge. Discussions during the grade-level or MTSS meetings with educators with diverse expertise will broaden the possible solutions described as plausible instructional techniques or intervention approaches to implement in response to the student concerns. This process of studying, sharing, and learning is so important to the development as action researchers as we investigate issues and possible solutions and share in new learning. Collaboration among educators within the schools provides knowledgeable resources and support during classroom implementation related to the instructional focus of the plan.

When selecting an instructional focus, the practices that are implemented should directly target the identified classroom problem. At times, the instructional focus may be determined at the school or district level (for example, instructional decisions about the purchase and use of a particular evidence-based program). In addition, when discussing the instructional focus, consider the specific proactive practices that help to ensure fidelity of implementation.

Identify Data Collection Sources

Data collection through continuous progress monitoring is a crucial step in the classroom instructional DDDM process and action research. Teachers continuously collect data to measure whether instructional practices have had the desired effect. The collected data provide information to answer the instructional questions related to improved student learning. In addition, the data collected provide critical feedback on the instruction or intervention plan for the students at each tier of the MTSS framework. DDDM within the entire AR process is based upon progress monitoring of student results in each of the three tiers.

Determine Level of Support

Educators frequently engage in classroom instructional DDDM processes with support from their colleagues, support personnel, educational agencies, or university faculty. During planning, it is important to consider needed information, resources, and support to ensure fidelity of implementation and continuous progress monitoring. See tables 5.6 and 5.7 for an example of the classroom instructional DDDM based upon the vignette of Ms. Hernandez and a template for use.

> Stop and Reflect:
>
> As you consider your own learning and knowledge to implement DDDM in your school, reflect on the following critical questions to determine possible sources of support for you as you implement the DDDM process: Do you need further professional development? Will you need assistance with data collection and analysis? Could working with an instructional coach provide you with the support needed to implement evidence-based instructional programs with high fidelity? Will having opportunities to discuss the resources, plans, or assessment probes with colleagues provide a needed support system?

Outline an Implementation Schedule

The final planning step is developing an implementation schedule, which lists the tasks to be completed, the beginning and ending dates for each task, and the necessary resources. This schedule serves as a timeline of activities during implementation of the instructional plan. One of the critical tasks to include is a follow-up meeting with the grade-level or MTSS team members, after several weeks of implementation, to review progress monitoring data. At that follow-up meeting, discussions related to the specific instructional and intervention plans are held to determine the effectiveness of the plan related to student outcomes as assessed through continuous progress monitoring. An example of an implementation schedule and a template are provided in tables 5.8 and 5.9.

Table 5.6. Example of a Classroom Instructional DDDM Plan

Classroom Instructional DDDM Plan
Name(s): *Ms. Hernandez* **School:** *ABC Elementary School* **Grade Level:** *First Grade*
Research Question: Pose a question that will focus your study. Be sure to include what student learning will occur and what instructional practices will be implemented. *How will incorporating visible prompts and hands-on manipulatives into small group reading instruction affect my students' ability to hear and record sounds in words and increase the identified sight words?*
Learning Outcomes: What specific student learning will occur? *The students will improve their letter/sound correspondence.* *The students will improve their ability to hear and record sounds in words (phonemic awareness and phonics).* *The students will increase the number of identified sight words.*
Instructional Focus: Describe the specific instructional practice(s) that will be implemented and studied. Specify when and how the practice will be implemented. *The students will receive small group reading instruction using an evidence-based program and resources following a systematic instructional plan, which includes daily word work that will incorporate the following teaching techniques and manipulatives:* - *Providing explicit instruction in developing letter-sound correspondence* - *Building the ability to hear and record sounds in words by incorporating Elkonin Boxes (tokens and letters) and other visible prompts into daily word work* - *Using letter magnets, white boards, shaving cream, and chalkboard/water for practicing building and manipulating words* - *Connecting reading to writing using an evidence-based reading instruction program*
Data Collection: Specify the data sources that you will collect that are aligned to the classroom problem. Describe how often you will collect the data. **Data Source 1: (What and How?)** *Letter-Sound Identification Survey, bi-monthly* **Data Source 2: (What and How?)** *Sight Word Identification and Phonics Survey, bi-monthly* **Data Source 3: (What and How?)** *Hearing and Recording Sounds in Words (Writing Samples, Observations), daily* **Data Source 4: (What and How?)** *School required reading and writing assessments, every nine weeks*
Support: What support will you need from your colleagues? - *Coaching and guidance from our literacy coach*

Table 5.7. Template for Classroom Instructional DDDM Plan

Classroom Instructional DDDM Plan		
Name(s):	School:	Grade Level:
Research Question: Pose a question that will focus your study. Be sure to include what student learning will occur and what instructional practices will be implemented.		
Learning Outcomes: What specific student learning will occur?		
Instructional Focus: Describe the specific instructional practice(s) that will be implemented and studied. Specify when and how the practice will be implemented.		
Data Collection: Specify the data sources that you will collect that are aligned to the classroom problem. Describe how often you will collect the data. **Data Source 1:** (What and How?) **Data Source 2:** (What and How?) **Data Source 3:** (What and How?)		
Support: What support will you need from your colleagues?		

Table 5.8. Example of Implementation Schedule

Tasks	Timeline Beginning/Ending	Resources
Investigate area of concern by administering informal assessment	9/1–9/5	Informal assessment surveys
Analyze informal assessments	9/8	Time and planning period
Consult with literacy coach for developing instructional focus	9/10	Analyzed informal assessments, time, and planning period
Locate materials for reading instruction	9/12–9/15	Resource teacher, literacy coach manipulatives, and books
Implement instructional focus	9/2–2/3	Reading materials, manipulatives, and resources
Monitor students' learning	9/2–2/3 daily, bi-monthly, and every nine weeks	Informal assessments, school required assessments, time for analysis, and planning period
Follow-up meeting	10/2	Time for analyses of continuous progress monitoring data to evaluate impact of planning

Table 5.9. **Template of Implementation Schedule**

Tasks	Timeline Beginning/Ending	Resources

Implement the Plan with Fidelity

This classroom instructional DDDM process of action research within the framework of the MTSS may represent a significant instructional shift for many educators. It requires a coordination of processes at both the school and classroom levels. Fidelity of implementation is critical for the classroom instructional plan to be successful. Therefore educators within districts, schools, and classrooms must advocate for the needed resources (for example, programs, professional development, time for planning) to ensure that evidence-based instructional programs and practices are implemented with fidelity to achieve improved outcomes for students.

During the implementation of the instructional or intervention plan in the classroom, it is important to implement the instructional practices with fidelity. Important considerations include the following.

Implement the instructional practices consistently. To maintain the integrity of your instruction, it is critical that implementation of the instructional practices and data collection occurs as described. Follow the plan as written.

Implement the instructional practices as they were designed to be implemented. Evidence-based instructional methods, strategies, programs, and routines have been developed using information gathered from much research on their effectiveness. Deviations from guidelines for use of instructional resources may affect the results within the classroom. Another way to ensure fidelity implementation is to obtain feedback and guidance from an instructional coach or another teacher who is knowledgeable in a specific instructional practice.

> **READ ALL ABOUT IT!**
>
> Reviews of evidence-based programs are published by the Institute of Educational Sciences at https://ies.ed.gov/ncee/wwc/Search/Products?Topic=3.

Monitor student results through continuous progress monitoring. Throughout this process, educators monitor student learning to determine if their teaching is having an impact. The collection and analysis of data related to student achievement determines whether the teaching techniques have been effective. In other words, it is the data collected and analyzed during this process by classroom teachers (and others, if appropriate) that provide the answers to the instructional concerns in classrooms.

As described earlier, ensuring the fidelity of implementation is critical at both the school level (for example, implementation of the MTSS process) and the classroom level (for example, implementation of both instruction and progress monitoring). Three dimensions that affect the fidelity of implementation within classrooms and schools include the following:

- Method: Various types of instructional programs and resources include various levels of support and information within them to facilitate classroom implementation (for example, scripted lessons and resources that include all necessary materials for instruction).
- Frequency: The opportunities for implementation, instructional coaching, and professional feedback vary. Factors such as experience, student characteristics, and schedules for implementation may have an impact.
- Support Systems: The availability of ongoing professional development and feedback during implementation may vary.

At the school level, resources to support teachers during implementation should be identified. For example, instructional coaches with knowledge of the specific instructional program may be available to model and provide feedback to the classroom teacher during the initial implementation of the program. In addition, behavior interventionists with specific data collection and strategies in behavior management can model strategies and collect observational assessment data as described in the DDDM plan. At the school level, administrators and members of the MTSS teams focus resources to ensure high-fidelity implementation. In addition, classroom teachers need time to plan (individually and with members of teams, such as grade-level and MTSS teams), time to analyze student progress monitoring data from instruction, and time to revise and redevelop resources to address identified concerns. School leaders can coach and/or facilitate instructional coaching of teachers in this process. Critical questions to focus this process of feedback during instruction include the following:

- How much time do students spend practicing what is being taught?
- How much direct instruction is used in a class period?
- Is reteaching determined by using reviewed student work?
- Which strategies are based on current research?
- How is the lesson aligned to state, district, and school academic goals?
- How do lessons support state standards?
- What measures are used to determine student success?
- Is progress monitored continuously?
- Is instruction clear and focused?
- Are there high expectations for all students?

Teachers can benefit from seeing other teaching environments and observing how their colleagues teach. School leaders can facilitate this by

- allowing teachers to exchange classes and teach from someone else's plans,
- providing release time to observe in other classrooms or schools,
- funding conferences and workshops to support specific school goals,
- providing planning time for teachers to share what they observe and learn, and
- recognizing teacher successes.

Specific instructional resources (for example, programs, curriculum-based assessments) should be identified and made available to classroom teachers. Continuous professional development, based upon topics identified by classroom teachers during the MTSS meetings, could be scheduled into the calendar of professional development offerings. For example, topics related to understanding available data (for example, results of state assessments, early literacy assessments, frequency data collection), use of a school-adopted reading program, and the DDDM process could be professional development sessions offered on a continuous basis. These sessions can be offered in large group professional development meetings, as well as reviewed and discussed during study groups on grade-level teams. See additional information regarding professional development in chapter 7.

Classroom implementation with evidence-based instructional methods based on the identified needs of students during the phases of DDDM process within action research and/or the MTSS framework has the potential to improve the results for all students. Teachers and other educators within classrooms and schools ensure the successful mastery of the instructional goals and behavioral expectations based upon data using the DDDM process.

EQUITABLE DDDM

As described in earlier chapters of this book, DDDM provides a continuous improvement model for teachers and other educators to integrate and focus instruction and interventions to the specific needs of students. DDDM can serve to (a) provide a process to identify and use various instructional practices and interventions; (b) facilitate increased implementation of effective EBPs, strategies, and resources; (c) monitor and document student progress through continuous progress monitoring; and (d) increase the speed, determination, and efficiency of potential, additional educational services needed by individual students to improve student learning. At any time that individuals are making decisions (such as in the DDDM process), there is always a chance for subjectivity, even if not consciously. This is one of the most critical components of equitable classroom practices and one that educators have the most control over. For diverse learners, subjective assessment and placement decisions have led to many of the inequitable outcomes described at the beginning of this chapter. These subjective decisions have often occurred when students have been assessed through observations, teacher nomination, and other "opinion-based" measures (Herzik, 2015).

Researchers have shown that teachers often judge students from CLD backgrounds as more likely to have a disability or warrant more severe punishments for mild infractions when compared to their White peers for the same academic profiles or behaviors (for example, Fish, 2016; Gilliam et al., 2016). One theory for why this repeatedly occurs is implicit bias. Implicit bias refers to assumptions made subconsciously about groups of people. Implicit bias is often upheld and continued systemically (Payne and Hannay, 2021) and can be traced back to the original formation of public schools. Throughout time, the students experiencing the worst outcomes have often been blamed for their perceived deficits (for example, families that do not prioritize education, races being less intelligent than others; Artiles et al., 2016). Most educators do not intend to treat their CLD students unequally; yet evidence shows that this is occurring. It is important that educators take intentional steps to remove implicit biases from their decision-making processes. Some first steps in doing so are to self-reflect and question the DDDM process while engaging in this work. Some questions to pose include the following:

- Am I implementing the decision-making equitably?
- Am I giving all of my students the same "benefit of the doubt"?
- Am I upholding high expectations across all students?
- How much of my data are anecdotal or "soft" data? Which sorts of data do I use/include to inform my decisions?
- Which of my classroom problems am I choosing to prioritize in the first place?
- Am I considering feedback and input from others who know my students such as family and community members?

> Stop and Reflect:
>
> In the vignette, Ms. Hernandez is observing some initial concerns for several of the students in her class. The use of multiple sources of data (for example, assessments, observations, reviews of student products) provides individuals and groups of teachers and other educators with information to identify an instructional concern, develop and implement an intervention plan, and collect and analyze results. Consider the students in your classroom and review various sources of data to identify an instructional concern. As you consider developing an intervention plan, review the examples and templates to identify needed resources and supports within your school to implement your plan to address the identified area of need.

SUMMARY

The DDDM process is integral to the MTSS framework as teams of educators collaborate to identify classroom concerns or issues, develop and implement solutions, collect and analyze assessment data, and reflect and share the results to determine next steps. Evidence-based practices and programs and multisources of assessment data are necessary resources to be considered by knowledgeable educators in this DDDM process. Teachers and other educators engage in the DDDM process on a daily basis by (a) collecting and analyzing assessment data during screening, (b) prescribing additional assessments to further diagnose the presenting instructional concerns, (c) monitoring the instructional progress, and (d) summarizing the outcomes for a specific period of time (for example, length of intervention, grading period, annual progress, etc.). By asking questions, collecting data, intervening, and continuously monitoring student progress, teachers, like doctors, prescribe instruction and interventions to meet the academic, behavioral, and social-emotional needs for all students using the cyclical process of DDDM within the MTSS framework through the tiers. This DDDM process is also used by teachers and other educators during the AR process. When educators conduct action research, they are deliberate about the data they collect, the decisions they make, and the lessons they teach. The foundation of action research asserts that educational problems and issues are best identified and investigated at the classroom and school levels. By integrating action research into classrooms and schools, findings can be applied immediately, and problems solved efficiently and effectively.

KEY TAKEAWAYS

Educators engage in the cyclical DDDM process to develop instructional and/or intervention plans to address students' academic or behavioral issues.

Developing and implementing an instructional or intervention plan has multiple components, including data analyses of various sources, review of curriculum and resources, development of an instructional focus, and identifying progress monitoring probes.

Instructional practices, intervention plans, and progress monitoring probes must be evidence-based and implemented with fidelity.

Collaborative and collegial support during implementation strengthens solutions and fidelity of implementation.

Teachers and other educators are the central to the DDDM and action research processes.

Where can I find more information about DDDM?

Resource	Description	Link
Visible Learning by John Hattie	Summary of research of EBPs	https://visible-learning.org/
National Center on Intensive Interventions	Numerous vetted resources (for example, presentations, videos, articles, etc.) to implement MTSS and DBI	https://intensiveintervention.org/tools-charts/overview
National Center on Student Progress Monitoring	Numerous vetted progress monitoring assessments and probes for use by educators	https://files.eric.ed.gov/fulltext/ED502450.pdf
What Works Clearinghouse through the Institute of Educational Sciences (IES)	Published reviews of evidence-based programs	https://ies.ed.gov/ncee/wwc/Search/Products?Topic=3
National Center on Intensive Interventions: Assessment Tools Chart	Reviews, summaries, and examples of various assessments within multiple tool charts for reading, mathematics, behavior, etc.	https://intensiveintervention.org/tools-charts/overview

REFLECTION QUESTIONS

1. Describe the rationale and use of the DDDM process within MTSS.
2. Describe the DDDM process within the tiers of MTSS.
3. Discuss the steps of the DDDM process.
4. Describe important considerations with fidelity of implementation.
5. Describe the connections between DDDM and action research.

CHAPTER REFERENCES

Artiles, A., Dorn, S., and Bal, A. (2016). Objects of protection, enduring nodes of difference: Disability intersections with "other" differences, 1916 to 2016. *Review of Research in Education, 40*, 777–820. https://doi.org/10.3102/0091732X16680606

Every Student Succeeds Act, Public Law 114-95, 114th Cong., 1st sess. (2015).

Fish, R. E. (2016) The racialized construction of exceptionality: Experimental evidence of race/ethnicity effects on teachers' interventions. *Social Science Research, 62*, 317–34. https://doi.org/10.1016/j.ssresearch.2016.08.007

Gesel, S. A., LeJeune, L. M., Chow, J. C., Sinclair, A. C., and Lemons, C. J. (2021). A meta-analysis of the impact of professional development on teachers' knowledge, skill, and self-efficacy in data-based decision-making. *Journal of Learning Disabilities, 54*(4), 269–83. https://doi.org/10.1177/0022219420970196

Gilliam, W. S., Maupin, A. N., Reyes, C. R., Accavitti, M., and Shic, F. (2016). Do early educators' implicit biases regarding sex and race relate to behavior expectations and recommendations of preschool expulsions and suspensions. *Yale University Child Study Center, 9*(28), 1–16.

Herzik, L. (2015). A better IDEA: Implementing a nationwide definition for significant disproportionality to combat overrepresentation of minority students in special education. *University of San Diego Law Review, 52*, 951.

Little, M. (2012). Action research and response to intervention: Bridging the discourse divide. *The Educational Forum, 76*, 69–80. doi: 10.1080/00131725.2012.629286

Payne, B. K., and Hannay, J. W. (2021). Implicit bias reflects systemic racism. *Trends in Cognitive Sciences, 25*(11), 927–36. https://doi.org/10.1016/j.tics.2021.08.001

National Center for Intensive Interventions. (n.d.) Retrieved from https://intensiveintervention.org/.

Sagor, R., and Williams, C. (2016). *The action research guidebook: A process for pursuing equity and excellence in education.* New York: Corwin.

Slanda, D. D., and Little, M. E. (2018). Exceptional education is special. In G. Hall, D. Gollnick, and L. Quinn (Eds.), *Handbook on teaching and learning.* Hoboken, NJ: Wiley-Blackwell.

Yendol-Hoppey, D., and Fichtman, N. (2020). *The reflective educator's guide to classroom research: Learning to teach and teaching to learn through practitioner inquiry.* New York: Corwin.

Chapter Six

Action Research Using Data-Driven Decision-Making within MTSS

INTRODUCTION

After gaining knowledge about action research (AR), multi-tiered systems of support (MTSS), and data-driven decision-making (DDDM), it is now time to explore how these components can be integrated. This chapter offers a thorough analysis of the integrated process, with a specific focus on the problem-solving process. The emphasis is on the continuous cycle that is crucial for effective instruction and intervention, resulting in improved student outcomes. Additionally, two case studies are presented in this chapter to enable the application of acquired skills.

The structure of this chapter deliberately deviates from the preceding ones. The purpose behind this approach is to acknowledge that you have received significant content and resources and obtained essential information that will empower you to effectively apply the skills you have acquired.

OBJECTIVES

After reading this chapter, the reader will be able to

- explain how action research, MTSS, and DDDM work together to improve student outcomes;
- analyze the collaborative decision-making process; and
- connect and apply action research, MTSS, and DDDM to case studies.

PUTTING THE PIECES TOGETHER

Educators possess exceptional expertise to meet the varied learning and behavioral requirements of students they encounter throughout their professional journey. Frequently, educators adeptly address the needs of students concurrently, consistently adapting their teaching methods and behavioral strategies in a responsive, fluid, and flexible manner. The capacity to promptly make decisions that are responsive to students reflects a problem-solving framework, a framework so inherent to educators that they may not even be aware of their active involvement in it. The education system has widely adopted a cyclical problem-solving framework that is evident in the incorporation of its elements in action research, MTSS, and DDDM, as discussed in the initial chapters of this book. By integrating action research, MTSS, and DDDM, a more robust approach can be achieved to meet the diverse learning requirements of students in an equitable manner.

FOUR PHASES IN THE THREE TIERS

The MTSS framework employs a three-tiered approach that utilizes DDDM across all tiers to enhance learning, behavior, and social emotional outcomes. As discussed in chapter 4, tier 1 provides core instruction to all students, tier 2 offers supplementary support and intervention to select students, and tier 3 provides targeted and individualized support to a limited number of students. At each tier, students receive differentiated instruction based on assessment data from universal screening, diagnostic assessments, and progress monitoring.

Within each tier, the four steps of the DDDM process can be utilized either at the student, classroom, or school level. The educator can ask: What is happening with my student? What is happening in my classroom? What is happening in my school? As previously described, the DDDM process consists of four phases.

The four phases of DDDM fit within the MTSS framework as illustrated in figure 6.1.

Despite their complexity, these frameworks embody the actions of effective educators in their day-to-day work. Likewise, DDDM and action research complement each other. Previously, action research was described as a systematic process where teachers critically evaluate their teaching methods and adapt them based on thorough analysis of their students' assessment data. Now let's explore how DDDM and action research can be considered at each tier. Table 6.2 provides an overview of how DDDM and action research fit within each tier.

Table 6.1. Phases of DDDM

Four Phases of DDDM	
1. Identify	Using data, identify student, classroom, or school-based area of need related to enhancing student outcomes
2. Develop and Implement	In response to the data, develop and implement an intervention plan using evidence-based practices to address the identified area of need
3. Collect and Analyze	After sufficient time for the intervention implementation, collect assessment data to determine if the evidence-based practices improved student outcomes
4. Reflect and Share	After reviewing the data, reflect on the results to determine next steps and share results with colleagues

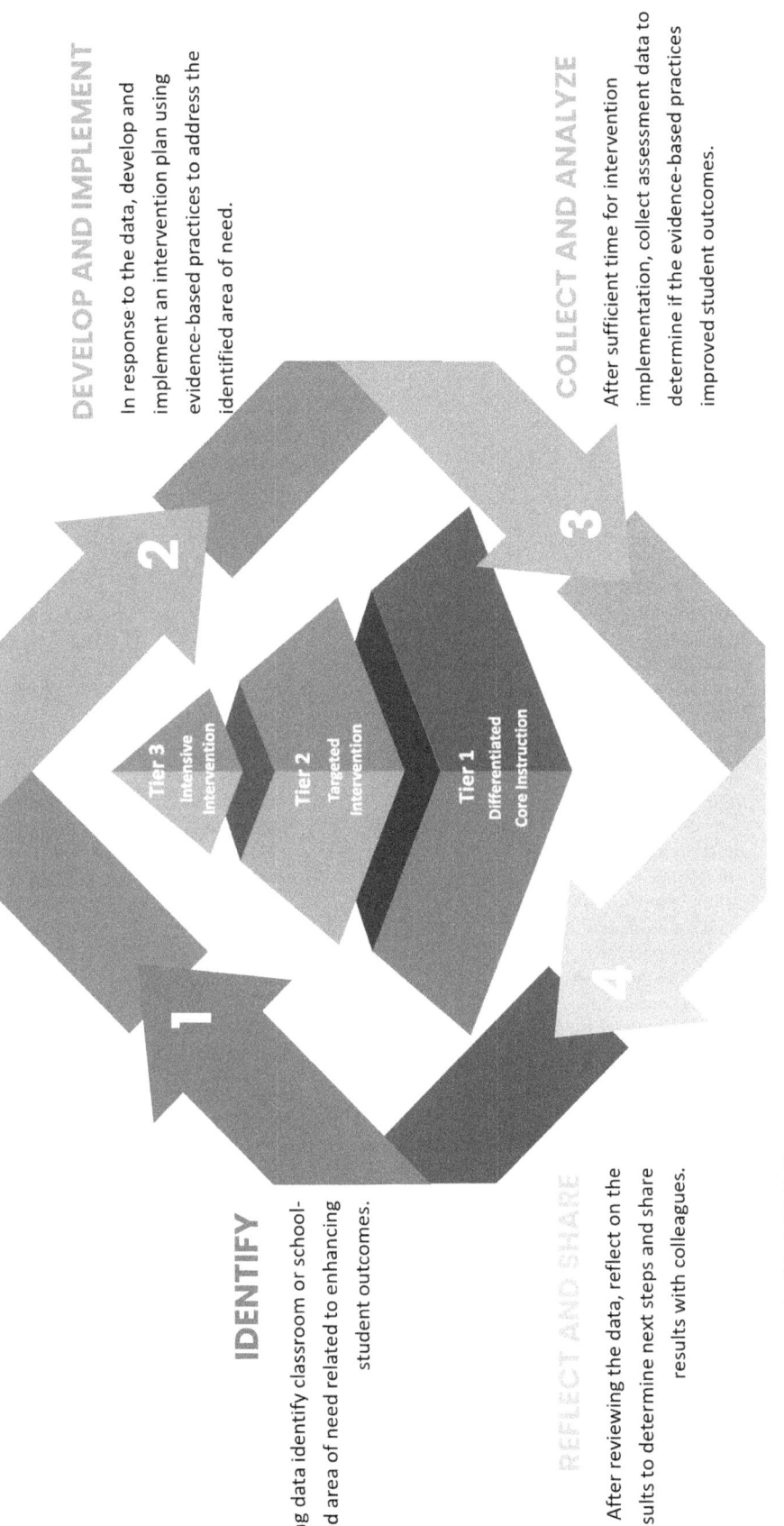

Figure 6.1. MTSS Framework with DDDM Phases.

Table 6.2. DDDM and Action Research across the Tiers

Tier	Identify	Develop and Implement	Collect and Analyze	Reflect and Share
Tier 1	• What is happening in the learning environment? • What are strengths or gaps in the curriculum? • Are the instructional or behavioral strategies meeting the needs of students? If not, what needs to be adjusted? • Which students need additional supports? • Will changing something in the environment, curriculum, or instructional/ behavior strategies meet their needs?	• Core instruction • Universal design for learning • Culturally relevant practices • Evidence-based practices	• Universal screening • Diagnostic assessment • Curriculum-based measures • Informal assessment • Formal assessment • Standardized assessment	• PLCs • Parent conferences • Department meetings • Professional conferences
Tier 2	• What specific skill is the student struggling with? • What instructional strategies or intervention can be implemented to assist the student in working toward mastery of the skill? • How will you know when the student has achieved mastery?	• Supplementary intervention • Targeted skill development • Evidence-based practices	• Progress monitoring • Graphs • Informal assessment • Formal assessment	• PLCs • Parent conferences • Department meetings • MTSS meetings • Professional conferences • Publications
Tier 3	• Why does skill mastery continue to be a challenge for the student? • What may be preventing the student from benefiting from intervention (for example, dosage, frequency, fidelity).	• Supplementary intensive intervention • Targeted skill development • Evidence-based practices	• Increased progressed monitoring • Graphs • Informal assessment • Formal assessment	• PLCs • Parent conferences • Department meetings • MTSS meetings • Student study • Eligibility meetings • IEP meeting • Professional conferences • Publications

INTRODUCING MIGUEL

In the subsequent sections of this chapter, knowledge and skills from previous chapters are integrated to practice the knowledge acquired regarding DDDM, action research, and MTSS. Make use of the resources provided in this book to apply knowledge and skills, review information from websites, make informed choices, and showcase learning. It will become evident that there isn't a single correct solution but rather multiple perspectives on how to address the case studies as presented.

Case Study: Miguel

INTRODUCTION

Student: Miguel
Grade: First
Age: Six

Ms. Hernandez is a first-grade teacher at Fairview Elementary School. She has been teaching for three years and is certified in elementary education. Fairview Elementary is a Title 1 school that has four additional first-grade teachers, a reading coach, and a reading intervention teacher. The school supports all students through a three-tiered MTSS model. To facilitate the implementation of MTSS, administration recommends grade-level teams participate in professional learning communities (PLCs) to engage in action research using DDDM processes to discuss and address instructional needs of all students.

KINDERGARTEN REVIEW OF RECORDS

Miguel is a six-year-old bilingual male and Spanish is the primary language spoken in his home. In kindergarten, Miguel qualified for ESOL services. His kindergarten records indicated that he had a great attendance record with few absences. Miguel's behavior and life development skills were satisfactory according to his report card. Miguel demonstrated difficulties with early reading skills.

Table 6.3. ESL Assessment Results

English as a Second Language Assessment Results	
Test	Results
Oral Language Proficiency Test	Fall: Score 6, Level A, Non-English Speaking Spring: Score 19, Level B, Limited English Speaking
Comprehensive English Language Learning Assessment (CELLA)	Speaking/Listening: Low Intermediate Reading: Beginning Writing: Beginning

Table 6.4. Results—DIBELS Assessments

Assessment Period	DIBELS Measures	Score
Assessment 1	Initial Sound Fluency	Score 0
	Letter Naming Fluency	Score 1
	Phoneme Segmentation Fluency	Score N/A
	Nonsense Word Fluency	Score N/A
Assessment 2	Initial Sound Fluency	Score 12
	Letter Naming Fluency	Score 10
	Phoneme Segmentation Fluency	Score 3
	Nonsense Word Fluency	Score N/A
Assessment 3	Initial Sound Fluency	Score N/A
	Letter Naming Fluency	Score 14
	Phoneme Segmentation Fluency	Score 30
	Nonsense Word Fluency	Score 15

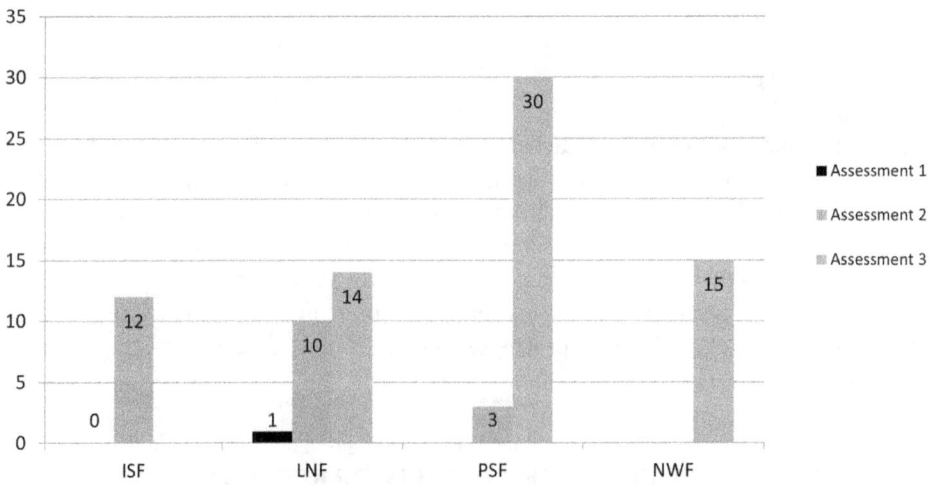

Figure 6.2. DDDM and AR Across the Tiers.

FIRST GRADE TIER 1 CORE INSTRUCTION

At the beginning of first grade, Ms. Hernandez administered various reading assessments along with the universal screener used within the school district. Ms. Hernandez reviewed the Assessment Period 1 data. She had concerns about several students with data within the Yellow and Red Success Zones, particularly the three students whose assessment data fell within the Red Success Zone. She planned lessons for the ninety-minute reading block that included whole group and small group instruction. The whole group instruction was guided by the core, evidence-based program selected by the school district to differentiate and support the various needs of students.

Period 1 Success Zones
Ms. Hernandez's First Grade Class

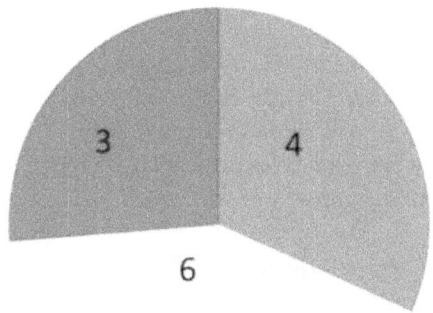

Figure 6.3. Class Assessment Results.

EDUCATION HISTORY

First Grade

Table 6.5. Results—Reading

Assessment Results: Period 1 for Miguel	
Probability of Reading Success	9%—Red Success Zone
Measure	Score
Listening Comprehension	4 out of 5
Vocabulary	29 percentile
Targeted Diagnostic Inventory (TDI) Letter Names	26/26, Met Expectation (ME)
Targeted Diagnostic Inventory (TDI) Letter Sounds	16/26, Below Expectation (BE)
Targeted Diagnostic Inventory (TDI) Phoneme Blending	7/10, Below Expectation (BE)
Classroom-Based Assessment	
Developmental Reading Assessment (DRA)	Instructional Level 2
High Frequency Words (Grade 1)	11/45
Quick Phonics Screener (QPS)	Letter Names—24/27
	Letter Sounds—13/26
	13/21 consonants
	0/5 vowels

Stop and Reflect:

Apply: Use the data for discussions by members of the PLC.
Using the data, describe the assessment results after the intervention. Consider the following questions:

- Was Miguel's response to the intervention positive, questionable, or poor?
    - *Positive* Response: The gap is closing, and you can extrapolate the point at which Miguel will come in range of peers.
    - *Questionable* Response: The rate at which the gap is widening slows considerably, but the gap is still widening.
    - *Poor* Response: The gap continues to widen with no change in rate.
- How is Miguel performing compared to others in the intervention group?

Discussion: Reflect on the assessment results. Consider possible next steps within the DDDM process for Miguel and the other students after receiving core instruction and additional supplemental instruction.

- What next steps would you suggest?
- Should any of the students be referred for additional, intensive interventions at tier 3? Why?
- Who else might need to be involved in the DDDM?
- Who should be included as part of the MTSS team to help support Miguel?

REFLECT AND SHARE: DECISIONS AND NEXT STEPS

Ms. Hernandez met with her PLC team to assist with examining the data. Ms. Hernandez and the team determined that Miguel had a limited positive response to the intervention. The team also recommended that Ms. Hernandez seek assistance from the MTSS team for additional DDDM to determine more intensive interventions based upon the assessment data collected for tier 2 interventions.

IDENTIFY THE INTERVENTION CONSIDERATION: TIER 2

The MTSS team was assembled. In addition to the core members of the team, the ESOL teacher, the reading coach, and the intervention teacher were added to the team. The MTSS team met with Ms. Hernandez to review and analyze the assessment data from Miguel's AP 1, AP 2, and progress monitoring data. In addition, the MTSS team members learned about the instruction and interventions already developed and implemented by Ms. Hernandez in the previous weeks as a result of DDDM with grade-level colleagues on the PLC team.

Apply: Problem Identification
Identify a problem statement(s) for Miguel.

Considerations:
- The statement must include behaviors that are measurable, observable, and reportable.
- Utilize this problem statement frame: Miguel performs at _____ when his expected level of performance is _____ as measured by _____.

DEVELOP AND IMPLEMENT: TIER 2

The MTSS team examined all of Miguel's data and developed three problem statements.

1. Miguel can read passage level 1.1 when his expected level of performance is 1.4 as measured AP 2 assessment.
2. Miguel can read at seventeen words per minute with 79 percent accuracy when his expected level of performance is ninety-seven words per minute with 90 percent accuracy as measured by Oral Reading Fluency.
3. Miguel can recognize eighteen out of forty-five high frequency words when his expected level of performance is forty-three out of forty-five words as measured by the first-grade high frequency word list.

Tier 2:

During the intervention period, the reading teacher works with the students on a daily basis five times per week for forty-eight minutes per day.

During this time, the reading teacher includes several strategy supports to assist struggling students with making progress. She incorporates a book club that allows students the opportunity to read text of their interest to assist with expanding word knowledge, background information, and increase reading abilities. She also allows students the opportunity to discuss what they are reading with their group buddies. When students are having difficulty during whole group instruction, she works to scaffold the learning during small group instructional time that focuses on reading and writing techniques. Instruction includes word study, reading fluency, vocabulary, and comprehension strategies based on student data results. She also includes shared reading activities and phonics mini lesson instruction to increase spelling.

COLLECT AND ANALYZE: TIER 2

Results of progress monitoring and diagnostic assessments for Miguel:

Table 6.6. Results—Diagnostic Assessments

Test	Progress Monitoring/Further Diagnostic Assessments	
	Score and Score Interpretation	
DAR	Print Awareness	6, Mastery
Diagnostic Assessments of Reading (second edition)	Rhyming Words	2/8, Nonproficient
	Segmenting Words	3/7, Mastery
	Hearing Initial Consonant Sounds	6/8, Mastery
	Hearing Final Consonant Sounds	5/8, Nonproficient
	Auditory Blending	3/5, Nonproficient
	Naming Capital Letters	18/20, Mastery
	Naming Lowercase Letters	19/20, Mastery
	Matching Letters	6/6, Mastery
	Matching Words	5/6, Mastery
	Writing Words	2/5, Nonproficient
	Word Recognition	Level 1-1
	Consonant Sounds	10/21, Nonproficient
	Consonant Blends	7/12, Nonproficient
	Oral Reading	Level 1-1
	Spelling	Level 1-1
	Word Meaning	Level 1

Stop and Reflect:

Apply: Use the data for discussions by members of the PLC.
Using the data, describe the assessment results after the intervention. Consider the following questions:

- Was Miguel's response to the intervention positive, questionable, or poor?
    - *Positive* Response: The gap is closing, and you can extrapolate the point at which Miguel will come in range of peers.
    - *Questionable* Response: The rate at which the gap is widening slows considerably, but the gap is still widening.
    - *Poor* Response: The gap continues to widen with no change in rate.
- How is Miguel performing compared to others in the intervention group?

Discussion: Reflect on the assessment results. Consider possible next steps within the DDDM process for Miguel and the other students after receiving core instruction and additional supplemental instruction.

- What next steps would you suggest?
- Should Miguel be referred for additional, intensive interventions at tier 3? Why?
- Who else might need to be involved in the DDDM?
- Who else should be included as part of the MTSS team or interventionists to support Miguel?

REFLECT AND SHARE: DECISIONS AND NEXT STEPS

Ms. Hernandez met with her PLC team to assist with examining the data. Ms. Hernandez and the team determined that Miguel had a limited positive response to core classroom instruction and interventions in the reading. The team also recommended that Ms. Hernandez seek assistance from the MTSS team for additional DDDM to determine more intensive interventions based upon the assessment data collected.

TIER 3

The MTSS team then proceeded to analyze the problem. The team began to form a hypothesis of why Miguel is not performing at the expected target level.

Stop and Reflect:

Apply: Problem Analysis
Create a hypothesis for Miguel's problem(s). What are the causes of the problem?

Considerations:
a. Determine the most likely reason(s) this problem is occurring.
b. Determine the skill strengths and deficits.
c. Discuss whether the problem resides in the instruction, intervention, curriculum, environment, and/or learner. Although we may not have all this information available in this case study, it is important to consider all the variables that may contribute to Miguel's performance.

Discussion: Given the assessment data provided and your expertise and resources, what intensive interventions and instructional considerations for increased frequency, supplemental interventions, and increased duration might you suggest?

The team moved to the next step of the DDDM process, which is developing an intensive intervention plan to implement in response to the data. They were careful to spend some time in this area because if the hypothesis is inaccurate it could lead to choosing the wrong intervention and valuable time would be wasted on implementing an intervention that was not appropriate for Miguel's needs.

The MTSS team determined that the most likely reason the problem was occurring was because the intervention needed to target Miguel's skill deficit in phonics/decoding. They formed the following focus for intensive intervention:

- If Miguel increased his ability to decode high frequency and blend cvc/cvce words, then he will be able to increase his fluency.

The MTSS team then proceeded to design an intervention that supported the problem analysis.

Stop and Reflect:

Apply: Intervention Design/Implementation
Design an intensive intervention plan for Miguel that supports the identified continued area of instructional need.

Considerations:
a. Consider the material/resources that are available for use to support the focus for instruction/intervention.
b. Determine if more time is needed.
c. Determine how, when, and where the targeted intervention will be provided.
d. Determine how support will be provided to ensure fidelity of implementation.
e. Decide how the student's caregivers will be informed, involved, or engaged in supporting the instruction/intervention.

COLLECT AND ANALYZE: TIER 3

Ms. Hernandez and the reading intervention teacher collected data frequently to determine Miguel's response to intervention.

Stop and Reflect:

Apply: Based on the intervention plan, determine what data you would collect. Use various resources within this book, including the "Tools Chart" from the National Center on Intensive Intervention at https://intensiveintervention.org/tools-charts/overview.

Considerations:
a. What assessment can be used for ongoing data collection?
b. How frequently should assessments be conducted?
c. What would be a good rate of progress?
d. What will be the decision rule to determine that Miguel's response was positive, questionable, or poor?

REFLECT AND SHARE: TIER 3

Ms. Hernandez collected data frequently to determine Miguel's response to intervention. The MTSS team decided to reconvene with Ms. Hernandez after two weeks on implementation of the tier 3 interventions to review the assessment data.

Stop and Reflect:

Apply: Based on your intervention plan, determine what would be possible next steps to share with the PLC/MTSS teams and Miguel's caregivers? If assessment data still did not show positive improvements, what additional services might be considered?

INTRODUCING KELLY

As described in preparation for the previous case study about Miguel, knowledge, skills, and resources from previous chapters are integrated and referenced to practice the knowledge acquired regarding DDDM, action research, and MTSS for this second case study. Similarly, make use of the resources provided in this book to apply knowledge and skills, review information from websites, make informed choices, and showcase learning. It will become evident that there isn't a single correct solution but rather multiple perspectives on how to address this case study as well.

Case Study: Kelly

INTRODUCTION

Student: Kelly
Grade: Tenth
Age: Sixteen

Kelly was diagnosed with a specific learning disability when she was in the first grade. Due to her family's employment changes, Kelly has attended five different school districts in various states. Often her custodial parent, Ms. James, has not been forthcoming of the services or academic records for Kelly when enrolling her at each of the preceding schools. In addition, her attendance has been an issue at most of her schools. Kelly is currently a tenth-grade student at Union Park Senior High School. Mr. Ortiz is Kelly's teacher in her literature class and is her faculty advisor. Various teachers have expressed concerns about Kelly's disruptive behaviors in their classes. Mr. Ortiz set a meeting with the school counselor and invited several of Kelly's teachers to attend, as well, for a meeting of their grade-level PLC.

REVIEW OF RECORDS

From the records available to the school faculty and counselor, it appears that Kelly is a sixteen-year-old, English-speaking female. In first grade, Kelly qualified for special education services due to a specific learning disability. According to the limited records available, it appeared that she received services for reading, specifically phonics and vocabulary, from a reading interventionist and special education teacher in first and second grades. At that time, records indicated that she had a great attendance record with few absences. Kelly's behavior and social development skills were satisfactory according to her report card. Despite early interventions, Kelly continued to demonstrate difficulties with early reading skills. There appeared to be no additional information in the cumulative file in subsequent grades for Kelly. This year, subsequent calls to her mother did not receive a response to date.

IDENTIFY: TIER 1 AND TIER 2

At this meeting of the PLC among several of Kelly's high school teachers and the school counselor, Mr. Ortiz led the discussion and DDDM process. Each of the faculty members in attendance commented that Kelly does not appear to be able to read or comprehend the content in the textbooks from their classes. She rarely finishes her work or turns in homework. The teachers commented that she appears to be able to do the work if she is on task and answering questions in class discussions. Although she is in several after-school clubs and activities, she is not very popular with her classmates.

For a specific example, Mr. Ortiz commented that he often lets students work together to finish assignments. During independent work time, Kelly works with another student on independent seat work. In the last couple of weeks, however, Kelly has been checking her makeup, looking at her phone, and calling out to others in the class for more than thirteen minutes instead of helping her classmate with the assignment. When her partner asked her to lend a hand, Kelly said, "Man, I don't get this stuff. Just help me out." The student continued working. When Mr. Ortiz noticed what was going on, he told Kelly to put the makeup and phone away and to get to work. Kelly complied, but five minutes later, she got out the phone again. On another day, Kelly fell asleep. Also, Kelly frequently asks to go to the bathroom. Each time, Mr. Ortiz lets her go. Kelly's mathematics teacher and science teacher agreed with the behaviors that they observed in their classrooms as well. Both teachers commented that when assignments in their classes needed to be completed independently, so Kelly's behaviors appear to be more evident in those two classes. As a result, she had been sent to the assistant principal's office twice in the past three weeks.

Stop and Reflect:

Apply: Use the data for initial discussions by members of the PLC.

- What is Kelly's observable level of performance?
- What specific assessment data are available?
- What specific and observable data could be collected using assessment tools from either the National Center of Intensive Interventions (NCII) at https://intensiveintervention.org/resource/behavior-screening-tools-chart or the Positive Behavioral Intervention and Supports (PBIS) at https://www.pbis.org/resource-type/assessments?
- Review the types of assessments in chapter 3. What additional types of assessments might the team members suggest to collect specific information about Kelly's behaviors in each of the classes?
- Based on the available data, what are some considerations for Mr. Ortiz and Kelly's teachers to support Kelly to address the identified behavioral concerns?

DEVELOP AND IMPLEMENT: TIER 1 AND TIER 2

The members of the PLC team and the school counselor needed to determine the specific amount of time that Kelly spends off task during class time in each of the classes and the instructional tasks at the time of off-task behaviors. In addition, there needed to be assessment information about Kelly's academic skills, especially in reading. This is important given the course expectations for reading and understanding content from textbooks in each of the high school classes. The school counselor would continue to attempt to contact Kelly's mother while also alerting the school MTSS team about the concerns to date. The faculty at the PLC meeting felt that much more information was needed about Kelly's reading and past academic records.

In the meantime, each of the three faculty members reviewed the resources provided from the PBIS Center at https://www.pbis.org/ and decided to develop similar behavioral expectations for all of their students in their classes to address working independently on assignments. Therefore classroom expectations were developed, implemented, and shared with the students. The teachers agreed to comment daily on the positive behaviors by the students that met the classroom expectations.

In addition, all three of the teachers agreed to provide instruction that was scaffolded and differentiated to meet the needs of the students during the forty-five-minute class period that included whole and small group instruction. The teachers commented that several additional students in their classes also struggled with reading the vocabulary and chapter contents in the textbooks. Several of the students in each of the three courses had difficulty completing the "Checking for Understanding" questions at the end of the textbook chapters. Kelly, along with three other students, were placed in smaller groups. Mr. Ortiz met with each of the students during independent work time, and especially Kelly's group every day for ten minutes during his class. The students' independent activities were differentiated to support specific areas of need and based upon the content of the unit.

COLLECT AND ANALYZE: TIER 1 AND TIER 2

The school counselor and behavior specialist observed in Mr. Ortiz's classrooms during the next three weeks in November. They also met with the other faculty members on the PLC team after several weeks of additional data collection from observations. (Please review the data collection resources from the Center websites included earlier and/or that are provided in chapter 3 on assessments.) They reviewed the data to determine if Kelly needed additional supports based upon classroom observations.

At the end of three weeks of implementation of the new classroom expectations and instructional methods, behavioral observations were conducted, and the number of redirections for Kelly was recorded during a thirty-minute interval, using the same data collection assessments and procedures. Figure 6.4 shows the number of redirections per thirty-minute observation during the weeks of data collection. In short, these data indicate that there was much improvement in reducing the number of redirections

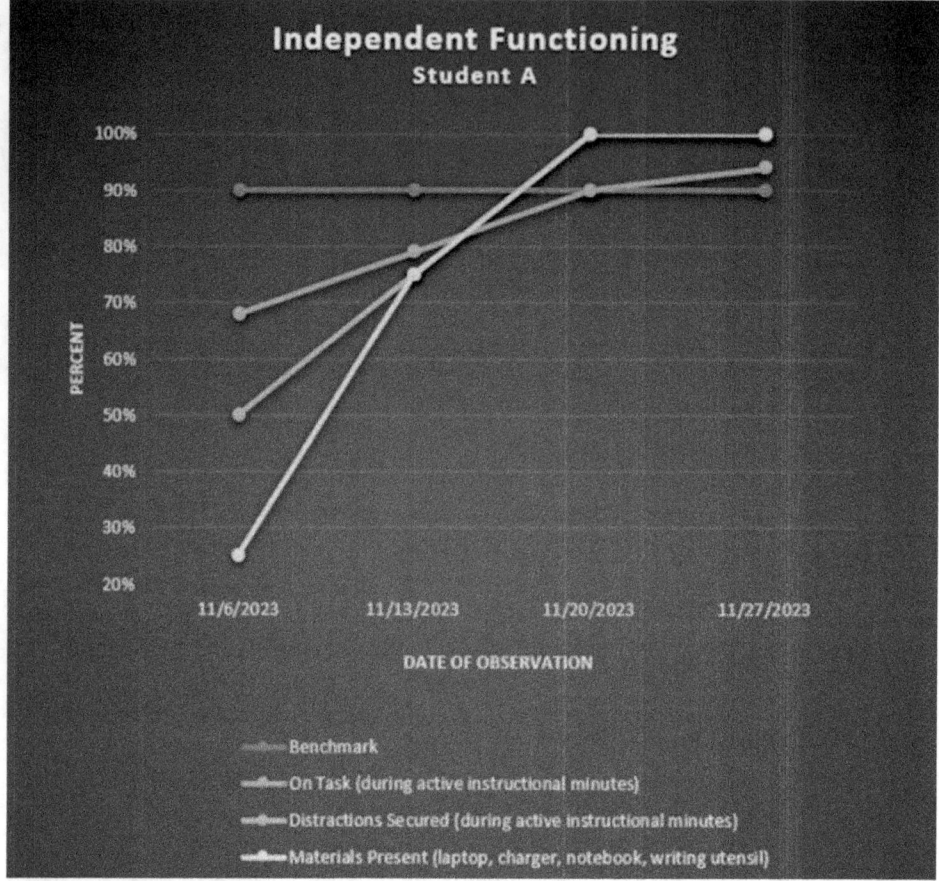

Figure 6.4. Data Display.

given to Kelly from the baseline period to the last week of data collection. Given these results, it is fair to conclude that the small group and differentiated instruction techniques, as well as development and reinforcement of specific behavioral expectations for the entire class, did have an impact on Kelly's behavior.

The team decided to continue the current academic supports and behavioral expectations, as well as continue to monitor her progress, both academically and behaviorally. They also decided to reconvene as soon as additional information was available for additional assessments and/or records, both as members of the PLC and the school-based MTSS team. Mr. Ortiz and the school counselor were members of the MTSS school-based team as well and could be liaisons with the grade-level teachers as additional information and interventions are made available. At this time, however, it appears that the interventions and plans enacted by the teachers appear to be addressing the concerns. Follow-up data collections and continued DDDM to continue to monitor the learning and behavior of Kelly were identified as well.

Stop and Reflect:

Apply: Use the data for discussions by members of the PLC.
Using the data, describe the assessment results after the interventions. Consider the following questions:

- Was Kelly's response to the intervention positive, questionable, or poor?
    - Positive Response: The gap is closing, and you can extrapolate the point at which Kelly will come in range of peers.
    - Questionable Response: The rate at which the gap is widening slows considerably, but the gap is still widening.
    - Poor Response: The gap continues to widen with no change in rate.
- How have Kelly's observed behaviors changed as observed and recorded on the graph?

Discussion: Reflect on the assessment results. Consider possible next steps within the DDDM process for Kelly to continue to receive additional supplemental instruction and specific positive reinforcement.

- What next steps would you suggest?
- What other observations should be conducted?
- Has Kelly met the behavioral goals during Mr. Ortiz's class as evidenced by the four observations during November?
- Should Kelly be referred for additional intensive interventions at tier 3? Why or why not?
- What additional concerns and/or information is needed?
- Who else might need to be involved in the DDDM within the MTSS team?

REFLECT AND SHARE: DECISIONS AND NEXT STEPS

Mr. Ortiz met with his PLC team to assist with examining the data from the four observations in his class. Mr. Ortiz and the team determined that Kelly has a limited positive response to the instructional changes and the intervention of explicit behavioral expectations for the entire class. The other two teachers mentioned that they believe that her behavior had improved but requested that the school counselor conduct similar observations in their classes as well to receive specific data from observations. The team also recommended that the team seek assistance from the MTSS team for additional DDDM to determine more intensive interventions based upon additional information provided by the parent and/or previous records, if received.

In addition, the PLC team also recommended that the members of the MTSS team determine specific assessment results in reading, specifically vocabulary and comprehension. The results of the assessments in reading should be shared with all of Kelly's grade-level teachers in a subsequent PLC meeting to further discuss and plan appropriate interventions, technology, and/or other instructional techniques to address Kelly's reading needs. The team also felt that these additional solutions may be helpful to other high school students in their classes who were not reading on grade level.

Stop and Reflect:

Apply:

- Who should be included as part of the MTSS team to support Kelly?
- What specific assessments in reading would be helpful to provide accurate information to plan for instruction within the DDDM process? Please refer to the NCII Academic Tool Chart at https://charts.intensiveintervention.org/aintervention.

IDENTIFY THE INTERVENTION CONSIDERATIONS: TIER 3

The MTSS team was assembled. In addition to the core members of the team, Mr. Ortiz, the high school reading coach, and the reading intervention teacher were added to the team. The MTSS team met with Mr. Ortiz to review and analyze the assessment data from classroom observations from November and progress monitoring data from various curriculum-based measurements from unit quizzes from the textbook. In addition, the MTSS team members learned about the instruction and interventions already developed and implemented by Mr. Ortiz and two of her teachers in the previous weeks as a result of DDDM with grade-level colleagues on the PLC team.

Stop and Reflect:

Apply: Problem Identification
Identify a problem statement(s) for Kelly.

Considerations:
a. The statement must include behaviors that are measurable, observable, and reportable.
b. Utilize this problem statement frame: Kelly performs at _____ when expected level of performance is _____ as measured by _____.

DEVELOP AND IMPLEMENT: TIER 3

The MTSS team then proceeded to analyze the problem. The team began to form a hypothesis of why Kelly is not performing at the expected target level.

Stop and Reflect:

Apply: Problem Analysis
Create a hypothesis for Kelly's problem(s). What are the causes of the problem?

Considerations:
a. Determine the most likely reason(s) this problem is occurring.
b. Determine the skill strengths and deficits.

c. Discuss whether the problem resides in the instruction, intervention, curriculum, environment, and/or learner. Although we may not have all this information available in this case study, it is important to consider all the variables that may contribute to Kelly's performance.

Discussion: Given the assessment data provided and your expertise and resources, what intensive interventions and instructional considerations for increased frequency, supplemental interventions, and increased duration might you suggest?

The MTSS team examined all of Kelly's data and developed three problem statements.

Kelly will remain on task in each of her courses observed with less than three redirections/class.

Kelly will participate with her team members and complete the "Checking for Understanding" questions to receive an 80 percent mastery.

Kelly will provide examples of each chapter vocabulary term and will receive an 80 percent on oral assessments by the teacher for each chapter unit.

The team moved to the next step of the DDDM process, which is developing an intensive intervention plan to implement in response to the data. They were careful to spend some time in this area because if the hypothesis is inaccurate it could lead to choosing the wrong intervention and valuable time would be wasted on implementing an intervention that was not appropriate for Kelly's needs.

The MTSS team determined that the most likely reason the problem was occurring was because the intervention needed to target Kelly's skill deficits in vocabulary and comprehension. They formed the following focus for intensive intervention:

If Kelly increased her ability to decode and/or recognize high-frequency and key terms, then she will be able to increase her comprehension.

The MTSS team then proceeded to design an intervention that supported the problem analysis.

Stop and Reflect:

Apply: Intervention Design/Implementation
Design an intensive intervention plan for Kelly that supports the identified continued area of instructional need.

Considerations:
a. Consider the material/resources that are available for use to support the focus for instruction/intervention.
b. Determine if more time is needed.
c. Determine how, when, and where the targeted intervention will be provided.
d. Determine how support will be provided to ensure fidelity of implementation.
e. Decide how the student's caregivers will be informed, involved, or engaged in supporting the instruction/intervention.

COLLECT AND ANALYZE: TIER 3

Mr. Ortiz, the school counselor, and the reading intervention teacher collected data frequently to determine Kelly's response to intervention.

Stop and Reflect:

Apply: Based on the intervention plan, determine what data you would collect. Use various resources within this book, including the "Tools Chart" from the National Center on Intensive Intervention at https://intensiveintervention.org/tools-charts/overview.

Considerations:
a. What assessment can be used for ongoing data collection?
b. How frequently should assessments be conducted?
c. What would be a good rate of progress?
d. What will be the decision rule to determine that Kelly's response was positive, questionable, or poor?

REFLECT AND SHARE: TIER 3

The reading intervention teacher collected data frequently to determine Kelly's response to intervention targeting reading vocabulary and comprehension. The MTSS team decided to reconvene with Kelly's teachers after two weeks on implementation of the tier 3 interventions to review the assessment data. Mr. Ortiz will be the liaison between the discussions and decisions by the MTSS team members and the grade-level PLC team. Continuous progress monitoring of the established goals for Kelly in behavior and reading will occur at least every two weeks. The guidance counselor collected the identified sources of assessment data and met with Kelly and her mother throughout this semester.

Stop and Reflect:

Apply: Based on your intervention plan, determine what would be possible next steps to share with the PLC/MTSS teams and Kelly's caregivers. If assessment data still did not show positive improvements, what additional services might be considered?

SUMMARY

The DDDM process is integral to the MTSS framework. As evidenced in the case studies, teachers collaborate with teams of educators to identify classroom and individual student concerns, develop and implement solutions, collect and analyze assessment data, reflect on the results, and determine next steps. Educators rely on evidence-based practices and multiple sources of assessment data throughout the DDDM process. This cyclical process provides a strong framework for teachers to identify both student strengths and opportunities for growth.

KEY TAKEAWAYS

- The cyclical DDDM process and action research approach can be integrated into the MTSS framework to address students' academic, behavioral, and social-emotional needs.
- Developing and implementing an instructional or intervention plan involves analyzing data from multiple sources, reviewing curriculum and resources, determining an instructional focus, and selecting progress monitoring assessments.
- Instructional practices, intervention plans, and progress monitoring tools must utilize evidence-based methods and be implemented with fidelity.
- Collaborative support during implementation includes PLCs, lesson studies, and team meetings.

Chapter Seven

Opportunities to Use and Share Action Research within Educational Settings

INTRODUCTION

This chapter focuses on the writing, implementing, and sharing of the action research (AR) findings. The most common and practical approaches for organizing, analyzing, and developing conclusions for different types of data are provided for different purposes and audiences. In addition, discussions about and examples of sharing the results with parents, other school-based educators, and/or the broader educational field through publications and presentations are described.

OBJECTIVES

After reading this chapter, the reader will be able to

- compare different ways to disseminate the results of action research;
- understand the importance of sharing the findings of action research with key stakeholders;
- understand the importance of ethical treatment of the research process, findings, and of participants in a study;
- analyze ways in which data may be shared collaboratively, including the use of professional learning communities (PLCs);
- develop a plan for how action research results are shared; and
- envision ways in which they may emerge as leaders through the dissemination of their research.

KEY TERMS

Professional learning communities (PLCs): A model of professional development that has focused on student learning for more than a decade and is implemented in many schools.

Lesson study: A cycle of instructional improvements focused on teacher collegial conversations based upon classroom observations during lessons.

Institutional review board (IRB): A group of research experts that has been formally designated to review and monitor research involving human subjects to make sure their rights and welfare are protected.

Family Educational Rights and Privacy Act (FERPA): Federal law that gives parents rights over their children's educational records, including control over the disclosure of personally identifiable information about their child.

VIGNETTE

Ms. Hernandez was pleased to have completed her action research and to see that many of her students did make gains on their reading/ELA scores. She felt that she had discovered an intervention that worked and was eager to share what she had learned with her colleagues. She met with her department chair, who suggested that she ask her principal about giving a presentation to the entire school on the next professional development day. Ms. Hernandez was unsure that she was experienced enough to lead a professional development session, but her department chair reminded her that she had something important to share and that others could learn from what had worked for her. She agreed to give it a try and got to work on creating a presentation that highlighted her efforts.

SHARING AND REPORTING ACTION RESEARCH RESULTS

After assessment data are analyzed related to established curricular goals and the instructional focus, it is time to share and report the results. Results can be reported in a variety of formats, depending on the audience and purpose of the reporting. Here are some options, some of which are described in more detail later in this chapter.

Individual reporting in student folders, files, portfolios, and other student records. This is probably the most common way results are reported within schools. Teachers complete an accurate report of the individual student's level of achievement of specific curricular goals. Data collected through the classroom instructional problem-solving process are easily reported through school, district, and state accountability reporting systems. This is why aligning the instructional plans to curricular goals is so important.

Written reports and professional articles. Teacher research continues to advance knowledge within the teaching profession. Reporting research disseminates important findings and advances the practice of education (Agasisti and Bowers, 2017). As an educator who has designed a research plan, implemented it, and collected student products (data) to determine its effectiveness, educators may describe findings through a report or professional article. Publishing and sharing the results of instruction is a form of professional development for others. The instructional plan and its implementation can be outlined in the elements shown on the template in table 7.1.

Discussions and presentations with other educators. A very effective strategy for disseminating action research results is using table discussions with other educators within grade levels, instructional teams, or the school. This provides personal professional development directly related to educational issues identified at the school. When presenting this information, report only on the expectations for the research study and present some of the data collected. Again, tables, charts, and graphs may be effective tools to use with the audience. Specific questions to facilitate dialogue include the following:

- Do you think that what I believe occurred is what really happened?
- As you look at the data, do you think any unplanned results occurred?
- In what ways do you think the quality of education for my students improved during this study?
- What did you learn from this study?
- What will be the next steps for you? For your students?

Discussions and presentations with families. Sharing your action research results should extend to the students (your participants) and their parents or families. This is important as families are key collaborators/stakeholders in this research, whether they directly participated or not. This is also an opportunity to initiate purposeful parental communication. Educators may want to send a letter home sharing the results of an effective practice they implemented or even just one student's progress. This sharing can help to strengthen school-home partnerships; parents will likely appreciate the interest that you are taking in their children's educational growth (Monem and Cramer, 2022). The students themselves, particularly older learners, have the right to see the outcomes of your work with them, and sharing these results might help them understand their learning better and perhaps cultivate their interest in inquiry. You may share information with families through letters home, parent-teacher conferences, or an open house night where you highlight research findings with families as a group.

Self-reflection and evaluation. Of course, the most important evaluation, reflection, and decision-making are completed by each teacher and educator involved with the process. The carefully planned and conducted classroom research results will provide new knowledge to make informed decisions about teaching and learning for all students. Once the data are compiled, analyzed, shared, and discussed, it is critical for teachers and educators to ask those core questions:

- How was the quality of education improved for my students?
- How has my understanding of my teaching changed and improved?
- Are my students meeting the academic and behavioral goals?

The answers to these questions will lead into the continued cycle of continuous improvement—creating new goals for improvement and plans for continued instruction and intervention based on evidence of student learning. As educators use their problem-solving abilities to address classroom needs through this process of classroom DDDM within the MTSS framework, students will learn, and educators can continue to grow as researchers and leaders within their field.

Stop and Reflect:

Think about ways you may consider sharing the results of your action research. Who may be interested in these results? Who may benefit from knowing your findings? What are the important contributions you want to make sure others know about this work?

SHARING DATA WITH KEY STAKEHOLDERS

Educators will likely learn a lot about their students and themselves by engaging in the AR process, but it is important that they do not keep this knowledge to themselves. Stakeholders such as colleagues, administrators, students, parents, and other educators are also invested in the important findings of their work. The sharing of information can lead to increased collaboration and, ultimately, a larger impact on the field and their class. Referring back to the high-leverage practices (HLP; McLeskey, 2017) from chapter 2, HLP 5 calls for educators to "interpret and communicate assessment information with stakeholders to collaboratively design and implement educational programs" (p. 19). There are many ways that you can share your research with key stakeholders, starting right within your own school and expanding to your community and the larger professional educational community.

SHARING YOUR RESEARCH IN PROFESSIONAL LEARNING COMMUNITIES

One way to share the findings of your action research is within PLCs, which are described as professional development models that focus on student learning and are implemented in many schools (DuFour and Eaker, 2009). The PLC model flows from the assumption that the core mission of schools is not simply to ensure that students are taught but to ensure that they learn. This simple shift (from a focus on teaching to a focus on learning) has profound implications within the schools. With allocated time, resources, and collaboration, every professional in the school engages in the continuous exploration of three crucial questions that drive the work within a PLC:

1. What should each student learn?
2. How will we know when each student has learned it?
3. How will we respond when a student experiences difficulty in learning?

To address these crucial questions, educators within PLCs recognize that they must work together to achieve their collective purpose of improving student learning. Similar to the DDDM process within action research, the powerful collaboration that characterizes PLCs is a systematic process in which teachers work together to analyze and improve their classroom instructional practices. Team members review assessment data and discuss current factors that may have an impact on the results. Planning for specific

> **READ MORE ABOUT IT!**
>
> Learn more about implementing PLCs: https://www.edutopia.org/article/creating-effective-professional-learning-communities/.

evidence-based practices and strategies to differentiate and/or intensify instruction and interventions may be considered. Knowledge and skills relating to current mandates, curriculum, and resources will improve the DDDM process within the PLC teams. During PLC meetings, the members of the PLCs share related, additional resources from professional readings, websites, and other sources. For example, information specific to evidence-based instruction and interventions may provide additional solutions to consider. These collaborative conversations and discussions enhance learning by all educators, as goals, strategies, resources, and results are shared.

Members of PLCs judge their effectiveness based on the results of students in their classrooms. When PLCs are adopted school-wide, every teacher as a member participates in an ongoing process of identifying the current level of student achievement, establishing a goal to improve the current level, working together to achieve that goal, and providing periodic evidence of progress. Part of this process may be developing or identifying common formative assessments that can be used to collect, analyze, and interpret the results of student learning. Throughout the school year, each teacher can then identify how his or her students performed on each skill. Individual teachers have access to the ideas, materials, strategies, and talents of the entire team, including other teachers and curriculum specialists. In addition, teachers on PLCs have support from their colleagues as they learn about and implement new ideas, materials, and strategies to meet needs of their students struggling to master the grade level content. PLCs are a model of sustained, job-embedded professional development for teachers to address the learning needs of their students to improve results. Through continued conversations of new learning and approaches PLCs offer an ongoing professional development structure to ensure continued learning for the teachers and other school educators to meet these goals based upon DDDM and critical inquiry.

Lesson study is a cycle of instructional improvements focused on teacher collegial conversations based upon classroom observations during lessons. Lesson studies provide an opportunity for feedback and learning about implementation of strategies, evidence-based instructional practices and/or interventions to address student learning needs by carefully recording teacher behaviors and student learning during the lesson. Within this process, a teacher colleague observes a designated lesson and collects and records teacher and student behaviors to share and discuss with other teachers after the lesson has concluded. The focus of DDDM in lesson study is the classroom implementation of instruction and/or interventions. In lesson study, this process includes the following:

- Form goals from student learning and long-term development.
- Study existing curricula, standards, and resources and discuss them related to the student results and possible adaptations and enhancements for differentiation.
- Collaboratively plan a lesson designed to meet both immediate and long-term goals for all students in the classroom.

- Teach the lesson, with one team member teaching and others gathering evidence about student engagement and learning.
- Discuss the observed information gathered during the lesson, using it to improve the lesson, the unit, and the overall instruction, including specific instructions for students who were struggling with the content of the lesson.
- Teach a revised and enhanced lesson, incorporating suggestions to teaching the lesson, for all the students, from the entire classroom of students to individual students struggling with content. Additional resources and new materials may be suggested and added to the revised lesson. (Lewis, 2009)

Through this cycle, teacher knowledge of content, instruction, and student learning is enhanced through the collaboration with other teachers. These opportunities deepen content knowledge of various curricula and standards, instructional methods and differentiation related to student responses to the lesson (Lewis, 2009). Lesson study focuses on the heart of the educational process: what happens between teachers and students in the classroom. Teachers and instructional coaches, as members of the lesson study team, meet continuously as a lesson study group. During observations as determined by the teacher, observational data are collected and shared with the teacher to improve teaching practices within the classroom. The goal is to enhance current teaching to the most effective and skilled teaching. Within MTSS, this goal is referred to as fidelity of implementation. In other words, observational data describe the teaching technique and/or instructional resource that was implemented as designed. Through this process, teaching using resources and evidence-based instructional methods and intervention practices continues to improve. Discussions of effective teaching practices, student engagement, evidence-based instructional practices and intervention programs, and formative assessment results are facilitated as we collect student assessment data, set instructional goals, and teach our students within a cycle of continuous improvement. This is an ideal setting in which to share the findings of your action research!

Creating portfolios showcases the learning and results of both teachers and students. A teacher's portfolio can serve many different purposes, depending on the professional goals of the teacher and the mandates of the school and district. As DDDM is implemented in conjunction with other school improvement initiatives, such as MTSS, data meetings, PLCs, and ongoing professional development opportunities (described earlier), the contents of a teacher's professional portfolio documents both the journey of change and learning, as well as the results from these changes. At any time, but especially when changes are implemented, it is very important to document and collect items that account for the impact of the actions, especially as related to student learning. Reflecting on student learning is one of teachers' greatest incentives and motivators. The professional portfolio serves to document the attainment of goals, both personal and professional, and to stimulate professional discussions and action planning.

Assembling items for a portfolio is a powerful vehicle for professional reflection and analyses. Various documents (for example, videos from lessons, lesson study planning documents, assessment results for specific curriculum units, individual student learning graphs) provide evidence of impact and effectiveness, as well as assessment data for professional growth and development. These artifacts also extend the scope of discussions to set new goals. Specifically, the portfolio contents serve as the data for the continued professional development of teachers. Logs of implementation, lesson planning documents, and video recordings of lessons provide current and accurate information to extend and enhance professional discussions covering all aspects of teaching.

Professional portfolios are not only used formatively with colleagues but can be used with continued professional learning for the development of teacher knowledge, skills, and competencies. Additionally, professional portfolios can be used as summative evaluation by principals and professional advancements, such as national board certification and/or another professional position. Indeed, the contents of professional portfolios can provide evidence of planning for instruction and interventions, interactions with students, feedback to students, student learning, and contributions to the school, district, and profession. Contents of the professional portfolio should be aligned with the professional standards and requirements of the school district, as available. Several suggested contents for professional portfolios include the following:

- Multiweek unit plan
- Instruction plan for a single lesson
- Samples of assessment procedures
- Knowledge of students and resources
- Video recordings of instruction
- Instructional artifacts of in-class assignments and homework
- Samples of student work

Therefore professional portfolios provide artifacts and data related to professional teaching and learning, the critical components of DDDM and school improvement, as directly related to student learning. These artifacts provide both formative and summative information to be shared with multiple audiences. With the implementation of DDDM in action research and MTSS, educators within schools and districts have a personal and professional responsibility to engage in professional development. Supportive, collaborative, and sustained professional development structures to learn about, implement, refine, and polish the necessary skills to implement DDDM within action research facilitate expert implementation. The learning that takes place can then be shared with others to support their learning and development. The educators who share their work with others can emerge as leaders within their schools and the field.

AR REPORTS AND PRESENTATIONS

When educators conduct action research as part of a college course or professional development experience, they are likely going to be expected to complete a report of the process and their findings and will likely be asked to share the results of their study with their classmates. This may be done through a formal presentation or a poster presentation. Table 7.1 highlights a sample format of how results may be shared in a report format.

Table 7.1. Sharing Your Results

Name of Teacher Researcher:

Name of School and County:

Research Site: *Provide a description of your school site. Details may include demographic information, number of students, grade level, specific programs or instructional methods being implemented, etc.*

Teacher Researcher(s): *Describe what grade level and content you are currently teaching. Provide information on specific professional development activities that focus on the stated instructional concern.*

Problem: *Provide a description of your identified classroom problem. How did you identify the classroom problem? Describe the students who were affected and possible causes of the problem. What were the goals for improvement?*

Research Process: *Provide a detailed description of your research process. What was your research question? What instructional strategies or practices were implemented that were aligned to the classroom problem? Describe your implementation.*

Data Analysis: *Provide a narrative summary of your collected and analyzed data. If appropriate, please include graphs and tables to accompany the narrative summary. Include templates of your data collection sources as well as student samples.*

Taking Action: *Provide a summary of your decisions based on your analyzed data. What are your next steps? Do you need to continue your plan using the same procedures? Do you need to revise your procedures? Were you satisfied with your results and ready to investigate new concerns?*

Professional Reflection: *What did you learn through this process? How did this process impact your teaching?*

Presenting Your Findings

There are many variations of ways in which educators can present their AR findings. This may be done through a video presentation or webinar. Often action researchers create a visual representation of their findings and put them together on a research poster that people are able to view. Whether the audience is the individual student or the district school board, charts, graphs, tables, and target lines describe the findings in a clear fashion. The presentation of data must be clear and meaningful. Confidentiality must be protected so that no one individual student can be identified. Computer-assisted software for analyzing, graphing, and charting data is readily available. One example of such software that is readily available to most educators is Microsoft Excel. When you visually depict your data, readers can easily see the story that your action research tells and better understand the trends of your findings.

When presenting these findings on a poster, researchers may be present alongside the poster to offer others the highlights of their work and answer any questions that others may have about the study. Another option is a comprehensive oral report about the study, usually accompanied by a visual presentation such as a slide deck where the presenter walks the audience through each of the steps of the AR process and highlights key findings. Regardless of the format, there are several points that would usually be covered in an AR presentation. See these points in table 7.2.

Table 7.2. What Should Be Covered in an AR Presentation?

- Statement of the problem or why your AR study was necessary (Why did you do this?)
- Brief description of what prior literature or studies have shown about this topic (What have others already done?)
- Research questions or the specific purpose of your work (What exactly were you trying to study or measure?)
- Description of your intervention (What did you do?)
- The specific results (What did you find?)
- Discussion of your findings (What do your results mean? What did you learn?)
- Implications of your findings (How does this impact your students? Your classrooms? Potentially other students and classrooms?)

Regardless of the type of presentation, it is important to consider the audience and any background knowledge they already have or may need to learn about your topic. Be sure to include visual representations of your data such as charts, figures, and tables as it makes it easy for the audience to understand your results or see patterns in the data without needing a lot of time to get into the nitty gritty details of each data collection point. Finally, be sure to allow time for the audience to ask questions they may have about your work. You are the expert on your own research! Your answers are important.

Sharing with the Profession and Educational Field at Large

Beyond sharing your AR findings with those in your school or local community, you can make a large contribution by more widely (and sometimes formally) sharing these results with other educational professionals. To reach a larger audience, you may consider sharing this research at a local, state, or national professional conference where you can share the findings of your work with other educational professionals and researchers. If educators have written a formal report as required by a professor or administrator, these reports can also be shared with stakeholders who have a vested interest in your results. Your findings may also be shared more widely so that other education professionals outside of your networks can benefit from learning about your work. This is often done by publishing your AR results in a professional journal that can be widely read by many.

Publishing Your Results

If your action research yields results or findings that would apply to other settings beyond your school or classroom, you may consider publishing your work in a professional journal that can be widely read by educators across the world to truly spread the impact of your work. In fact, there are some educational journals that specifically seek to publish educational action research. In addition to action research–focused journals, you may consider subject area–specific journals to publish your work. You may also choose your journal based on the school or grade level of your students. See table 7.3 for information on potential journals for publishing your work. Each journal has its own specific set of guidelines that it is important to follow, but some common features exist across many educational journals. Generally, articles are written following the writing

Table 7.3. Potential Publication Outlets for AR Articles

Journal	Topic Area	Link to Website
Journal of Teacher Action Research	General action research	http://www.practicalteacherresearch.com
Educational Action Research	General action research	https://www.tandfonline.com/journals/reac20
Remedial and Special Education	Special education	https://journals.sagepub.com/home/rse
Journal of Literacy Research	Reading/literacy	https://journals.sagepub.com/home/jlr
Middle School Journal	Middle-level education	https://www.amle.org/wp-content/uploads/2021/02/MSJ_Guidelines_2021.pdf

conventions of the American Psychological Association (APA), which offers specific guidelines for how professional papers should be written. They publish a manual titled *Publication Manual of the American Psychological Association*, which is currently in its seventh edition. The manual is highly recommended if you plan to write up a formal article or even for use in writing papers for graduate schools. However, Purdue University's Online Writing Lab has an excellent website that provides critical information about APA formatting for free (see https://owl.purdue.edu/owl/research_and_citation/apa_style/apa_style_introduction.html).

The key parts of any research article generally mirror the sections of the presentation outlined earlier. In an article, you would include an introduction; a literature review; a methods section in which you describe your participants, your intervention, and how you analyzed your data; a results section; and a discussion section. Again, as each journal has its own specific requirements, it is important to carefully review the submission guidelines. It is also a good idea to consult with a professor or someone else who has experience in writing this sort of paper to be sure you are adhering to professional standards. If presenting or publishing your work is something you are interested in but feel confused about where to start, keep in mind that many educational journals and professional conferences are hosted by professional educational organizations and most professional organizations provide presentation and publication opportunities.

Professional Organizations

Many professional organizations exist in every field of education. These generally offer memberships for a fee each year (often discounted for students), and the membership may include access to journals that are produced by the organization, professional development resources, discounts to professional conferences, and networking opportunities. Additional benefits that come from joining a professional organization may include awards that are given to members, opportunities to get involved in leadership within the organization, and potential additions to your résumé. Many organizations have local, state, or regional branches that may allow you to get connected and publish or present your work within less competitive venues. Many also have specialized subdivisions that could allow you to network with others who share very specific interests with your or get you involved in policy or advocacy work if that is your interest. For example, the Council for Exceptional Children has special interest divisions such as the Division on Autism and Developmental Disabilities and the Division for Learning Disabilities, among others. The International Literacy Association has special interest groups such as Children's Literature and Reading and District Literacy Leadership.

Websites for professional organizations often include information about upcoming conferences, resources and links for educators, and readings of interest to the field. If you are an educator with an interest in educational research, there are many benefits to becoming part of a professional organization. The organization will likely host a conference at which you may choose to submit a proposal to present your action research and produce a journal, magazine, or blog to which you may choose to submit a publication about your action research. Some professional organizations more broadly cover education and others focus on particular subject areas or age groups. Some of the more popular educational professional organizations can be found in table 7.4.

Special Consideration: Institutional Review Board

If you are planning to publish the findings of your action research, or if you are a student at a university that requires publications, you may need to complete a formal review process to gain approval from an institutional review board (IRB). The IRB is a group of expert researchers who ensure that any research being conducted is using ethical treatment toward human subjects (in the case of action research, your subjects or participants are likely the students in your class or school). If the action

Table 7.4. Educational Professional Organizations

Subject Area	Organization	Link to Website
Administration	The School Superintendents Association	https://www.aasa.org
Early Childhood	National Association for the Education of Young Children	https://www.naeyc.org
English	National Council of Teachers of English	https://ncte.org
General/ Curriculum	Association for Supervision and Curriculum Development	https://www.ascd.org
Math	National Council of Teachers of Mathematics	https://www.nctm.org
Middle School	Association for Middle Level Educators	https://www.amle.org
Reading	International Literacy Association	https://www.literacyworldwide.org
School Counseling	American Counseling Association	https://www.counseling.org
School Psychology	National Association of School Psychologists	https://www.nasponline.org
Science	National Science Teachers Association	https://www.nsta.org
Social Studies	National Council for the Social Studies	https://www.socialstudies.org
Special Education	Council for Exceptional Children	https://exceptionalchildren.org
Speech/ Language Pathology	American Speech-Language-Hearing Association	https://www.asha.org

research you are conducting is part of the typical educational practices that one would expect to take place in your class or school, your research will likely be exempt from this formal process. The US Department of Health and Human Services provides a flowchart to assist in what types of research would require IRB approval (https://www.hhs.gov/ohrp/regulations-and-policy/decision-charts-2018/index.html). One exemption in this chart is "research conducted in established or commonly accepted educational settings, involving normal education practices," which in many cases applies to action research. However, if your university or school district deems this process necessary, teachers would be expected to comply with these regulations. Whether a formal IRB process is completed or not, it is important to protect the rights and anonymity of students by being careful not to share identifying or sensitive information about them with others when you share your data. Be careful to keep data aggregated in a way that one could not figure out the participant(s) by personal information such as names and other information. It is also important to be familiar with Family Educational Rights and Privacy Act (FERPA) regulations. FERPA is a federal law that gives parents rights over their children's educational records, including the right to access their children's educational records, the right to have these records amended, and the right to have control over the disclosure of personally identifiable information about their child. See https://studentprivacy.ed.gov for more information about this important law.

> Stop and Reflect:
>
> Which professional organizations do you already belong to (if any)? What are some that you may want to learn more about and potentially join? Are there data you are collecting on your students that may be of interest to the larger educational field? How may you want to share this information?

LEVERAGING MTSS, DDDM, AND ACTION RESEARCH TO BECOME EDUCATIONAL LEADERS

Through continued collaboration, discussions of findings, and learning, student outcomes will improve. Importantly, each teacher and school-based educator is also emerging as a leader and advocate within the field of education. Educational leadership is not limited to those in formal administrative roles (for example, principal, assistant principal, department chairperson). Educators who are recognized for their professionalism, collegiality, ongoing learning, and contributions can often take on important roles as leaders among their peers.

Proactive Professional Development

Without a comprehensive blueprint for school districts to follow at this time, it is critical that educators take a proactive role in the establishment, continuation, or improvement of MTSS as both an early intervention and a data collection process that can add important information about student learning and progress. The success of MTSS will depend, to a great extent, on whether it is executed by highly trained professionals who have a firm understanding of the process.

Keep current with reading professional literature about best practices in the field. The resources and articles at the end of this section are helpful for solidifying your ongoing professional learning.

Attend professional developments at local, regional, and state levels as they are made available to you. Campaign for others to join you, including other teachers, reading specialists, school psychologists, and administrators.

Contact local Regional Resource Centers for up-to-date research information and model schools in your area.

Examine current school methods and programs to determine if any recommended or already used commercial programs are a good overall match. Review the criteria for instructional materials, products, and resources to be considered as "evidence based." Compare the current resources and instructional materials used against the published criteria.

Share expertise in instructional methods and strategies used to teach struggling students. Collaboration with other faculty and staff members will be key to successful school implementation of problem-solving approaches.

Promote the use of evidence-based assessments as data sources to monitor the MTSS and determine whether it is being implemented successfully.

USING YOUR DATA TO BECOME AN EDUCATION LEADER AND ADVOCATE

READ MORE ABOUT IT!

Learn more about teacher leadership standards: https://www.nnstoy.org/teacher-leader-model-standards/.

In 2008, the Teacher Leadership Exploratory Consortium was formed to develop model standards for teacher leadership. These standards were designed to encourage a discussion among professionals about teachers' leadership competencies that can be used alongside formal administrative leaders to promote good teaching and student learning. According to Harrison and Killion (2007), standards such as these can be used to ensure that teachers are prepared to assume important leadership roles outside of formal administration, such as resource providers, instructional specialists, curriculum specialists, learning facilitators, mentors, school team leaders, and data coaches. Seven formal domains were established across the various components of teacher leadership. Specifically relevant to this chapter are Domain V: Promoting the Use of Assessments and Data for School and District Improvement and Domain VII: Advocating for Student Learning and the Profession. According to Domain V:

> The teacher leader is knowledgeable about current research on classroom- and school-based data and the design and selection of appropriate formative and summative assessment methods. The teacher leader shares this knowledge and collaborates with

colleagues to use assessment and other data to make informed decisions that improve learning for all students and to inform school and district improvement strategies. As such, the teacher leader:

> Increases the capacity of colleagues to identify and use multiple assessment tools aligned to state and local standards;
> Collaborates with colleagues in the design, implementation, scoring, and interpretation of student data to improve educational practice and student learning;
> Creates a climate of trust and critical reflection in order to engage colleagues in challenging conversations about student learning data that lead to solutions to identified issues; and
> Works with colleagues to use assessment and data findings to promote changes in instructional practices or organizational structures to improve student learning. (Smylie, 2010, p. 45)

Stop and Reflect:

Think about ways this newfound data collection and analysis expertise may leverage you as a teacher-leader, especially through your collaboration and sharing of results. How can you leverage your findings to promote educational change in practices or organizational structures? Through this, how can you serve as an advocate for your students and your profession?

Domain VII of the standards, Advocating for Student Learning and the Profession, states:

> The teacher leader understands how educational policy is made at the local, state, and national level as well as the roles of school leaders, boards of education, legislators, and other stakeholders in formulating those policies. The teacher leader uses this knowledge to advocate for student needs and for practices that support effective teaching and increase student learning and serves as an individual of influence and respect within the school, community, and profession. The teacher leader:
>
> a) Shares information with colleagues within and/or beyond the district regarding how local, state, and national trends and policies can impact classroom practices and expectations for student learning;
> b) Works with colleagues to identify and use research to advocate for teaching and learning processes that meet the needs of all students;
> c) Collaborates with colleagues to select appropriate opportunities to advocate for the rights and/or needs of students, to secure additional resources within the building or district that support student learning, and to communicate effectively with targeted audiences such as parents and community members;
> d) Advocates for access to professional resources, including financial support and human and other material resources, that allow colleagues to spend significant time learning about effective practices and developing a professional learning community focused on school improvement goals; and
> e) Represents and advocates for the profession in contexts outside of the classroom. (Smylie, 2010, p. 47)

Think about how DDDM within action research can leverage this work as an action researcher and now teacher-leader to be an advocate. How can becoming more involved in the broader educational community through professional organizations, conferences, and networking advance your ability to impact change in your school and community? How might educational policy be impacted by the findings of your work? As an educator, you have an important voice. When you have well-collected data and well-shared findings to back up your recommendations, your voice holds more weight. Be sure to use your voice as the expert researcher you are becoming to advocate for what you are learning works for your students.

Stop and Reflect:

In the vignette, Ms. Hernandez was preparing to lead a professional development for her colleagues. Think about what you have learned about educational data that you have collected that you can share with colleagues to more widely improve educational outcomes in your school or the field. List three potential people or sources with whom you can share this information.

SUMMARY

Educators who conduct action research have many opportunities to share the results of this work. These range from self-reflection to sharing with key stakeholders, ranging from direct colleagues to the field at large, and should also include sharing findings with students and their families. Educator-researchers can also leverage their important work as classroom researchers to serve as advocates and leaders within educational communities.

KEY TAKEAWAYS

Classroom research findings are important and should be shared with relevant stakeholders.

There are multiple ways to share findings in many venues, including with colleagues in schools and through more formal venues such as professional presentations and publications.

Professional organizations can be a great way to stay connected to professional development as well as to disseminate action research and findings through conference presentations or journal articles.

Teachers and other school-based educators have the potential to leverage the sharing of your work to advance as a teacher-leader, regardless of formal position in schools and districts.

Where can I find more information about disseminating this work?

Resource	Description	Link
Microsoft Support	This site will give you step-by-step guidance to graph and chart your data results.	https://support.microsoft.com/en-us/office/video-create-a-chart-4d95c6a5-42d2-4cfc-aede-0ebf01d409a8
How to Create a Research Poster	This site hosted by New York University provides guides and examples for creating a research poster for presentation.	https://guides.nyu.edu/posters
Illuminate Ed Blog	This site gives practical and detailed advice about sharing research results with parents.	https://www.illuminateed.com/blog/2020/01/sharing-assessment-results-with-parents-families/

REFLECTION QUESTIONS

1. Describe the key stakeholders with whom you should consider sharing your action research.
2. Compare the different formats in which the findings of your action research can be shared with others.
3. Evaluate the impact that PLCs and other professional development efforts can have on collaboration and dissemination.
4. Reflect on how using action research may empower you to be an educational leader.

REFERENCES

Agasisti, T., and Bowers, A. J. (2017). Data analytics and decision-making in education: Towards the educational data scientist as a key actor in schools and higher education institutions. In G. Johnes, J. Johnes, T. Agasisti, and L. López-Torres (Eds.), *Handbook of contemporary education economics* (pp. 184–210). Edward Elgar Publishing.

American Psychological Association. (2020). *Publication manual of the American Psychological Association 2020: The official guide to APA style*. Seventh edition. American Psychological Association.

DuFour, R., and Eaker, R. (2009). *Professional learning communities at work: Best practices for enhancing students' achievement*. Solution Tree Press.

Harrison, C., and Killion, J. (2007). Ten roles for teacher leaders. *Teachers as Leaders, 65*(1), 74–77.

Lewis, C. (2009). What is the nature of knowledge development in lesson study? *Educational Action Research, 17*(1), 95–110.

Monem, R., and Cramer, E. D. (2022). Utilizing action research to integrate curriculum, instruction, and assessment in middle school classrooms. *Middle School Journal, 53*(3), 5–14.

McLeskey, J., Council for Exceptional Children, and Collaboration for Effective Educator Development, Accountability and Reform. (2017). *High-leverage practices in special education*. Arlington, VA: Council for Exceptional Children.

Smylie, M. (2010). *Teacher leader model standards teacher leadership exploratory consortium*. United States: teacherleaderstandards.org.

Index

Page locators in italics indicate figures.

accountability, 35–36
action research (AR), vii: approaches to, 10, *11*; benefits of, 9; compared with traditional research, *6*; considerations for, 12, *13*; culturally sustaining, 23–25, *24*; DDDM within process, 85–93; decision-making in classrooms, 3–4; defined, x, 1, 6; guidelines for successful implementation, 14; and institutional review board (IRB), 120, 129–30; locating further information, *15*; opportunities to use and share within educational settings, xiii, 119–34; origins and models of, 7–9; as planned inquiry, 7–8; practical application of, 1–16; types of research, 4–6; using data-driven decision-making within MTSS, xiii, 97–117
action research using data-driven decision-making within MTSS, xiii, 97–117; case study: Kelly, 109–16; case study: Miguel, 101–9; four phases in three tiers, 98, *98–100, 102*; key takeaways, 117; putting pieces together, 97–98; review of records, 101, *101, 102,* 109–10; Tier 1 considerations and implementation, 102, *103,* 110–14; Tier 2 considerations and implementation, 104–7, *106,* 110–14, *112*; Tier 3 considerations and implementation, 107–8. *See also* multi-tiered system of supports (MTSS)

American Psychological Association (APA), 128
assessments, 7; benchmark, 37; culturally sustaining, 43; curriculum-based assessment (CBA), 33, 48; diagnostic, 33–34, *42*; diagnostic assessment in academics, 39, *40*; diagnostic assessment in behavior, 40–41; direct, 83; ensuring equity in, 41–43; formal, 35–36; formative, 34, 39, 123; four types of, 37–41, *42, 53–54, 75,* 76–86; functional behavioral assessment (FBA), 34, 40–41; and observations, 43–47, *43–47*; standardized student testing, 35–36, *38*; summative, 34, 41
asset-based pedagogies, 17, 23

behavior: data collection for, *43–46*; diagnostic assessment in, 40–41; functional behavioral assessment (FBA), 34, 40–41; positive behavioral interventions and supports (PBIS), 20, 40–41; replacement, 34, 40; target, 34, 40
benchmark assessments, 37
Broughton, A. J., 18, 26
Brusnahan, Stansberry, 26

CEEDAR Center, 59
collaborative action research, 10, *11*
collaboration among diverse educators, 9
connections across disciplines, ix–x

continuous improvement, 3, 6–7, 8, 12, 14; and assessment data, 35, 37, 38, 43, 44, 49, 52–53; and multi-tiered system of supports, 59, 65, 74, 80–85, *86,* 87–88, *90,* 92

core curriculum, 58–59, 61

Council for Exceptional Children, 23, 26, 129

COVID-19 pandemic, viii

Cramer, E. D., 26

Crenshaw, Kimberlé, 19

critical consciousness decision-making (CCDM) model, 18, 26

culturally and linguistically diverse (CLD) backgrounds, 17, 18, 19, 22, 94

culturally relevant pedagogy, 18, 21, 22

culturally responsive teaching, 18, 21

culturally sustaining action research, 23–25, *24*

culturally sustaining pedagogy, 18, 21, 22

cultural statuses, 19

curriculum, instruction, and assessment, 82–83

curriculum-based assessment (CBA), 33, 48

curriculum-based measures (CBM), 33, *39, 48,* 48–50; key components, 49

data-based individualization (DBI), 1

data collection and analysis, xii, 33–55; curriculum-based assessment (CBA), 33, 48; curriculum-based measures (CBM), 33, *39, 48,* 48–50; and DDDM, 82–84; diagnostic assessment in academics, 39, *40*; diagnostic assessment in behavior, 40–41; diagnostic assessments, 33–34, *42*; ensuring equity in assessment, 41–43; formative assessments, 34, 39, 123; four types of assessments, 37–41, *42, 53–54, 75,* 76–86; functional behavioral assessment (FBA), 34, 40–41; guidelines for use and implementation, 52; guiding questions for reviews, *38;* key takeaways, 53–54; key terms, 33–34; and MTSS framework, 51–53; observations, 43–47, *43–47;* to plan instruction, 50–52; practical guidelines for classroom assessments, 43–52; progress monitoring, 34, *38, 42;* replacement behavior, 34, 40; summative assessment, 34, 41; target behavior, 34, 40; templates, 39, *40;* Tier 2, *106;* understanding purposes and types of assessment, 35–36, *36;* universal screening, 34, 37, *38, 42;* with various assessments, 83; work sample analyses, *47,* 47–48

data-driven decision-making (DDDM) process, vii, ix–x, xiii, 1, 73–96; action research (AR) within MTSS, xiii, 97–117; action research (AR) within process, 85–93; and assessment data, 35; collecting and analyzing data, 82–84; considerations for, 12, *13;* as continuous improvement model, 3, 6–7, 8; data collection with various assessments, 83; define learner outcomes, 87, *89, 90;* determine level of support, 88, *89;* develop instructional focus, 87, *89, 90;* development and implementation, 80–82, *98;* and equitable education, 93–94; fidelity of implementation, 73, 80, 91–93; four steps within, 4, *5,* 7, 8, 23, *53–54, 65, 75,* 76–85; high-quality classroom implementation with fidelity, 80, 81; identify data collection sources, 87–88, *89, 90;* identifying area of need, 76–79, *77, 78, 79;* implementing, 74–75; key takeaways, 85; key terms, 73; locating further information, *95;* next steps for, xi–xii; outline implementation schedule, 88, *89, 90, 91;* pose research question, 86–87, *89, 90;* problem statement, 78; progress monitoring, 80, 81–82; reflection and sharing professional learning, 84–85, 116; reflective questions, 83, *86;* triangulation, 73, 83

Deno, Stanley, 49

develop instructional focus, 87, *89, 90*

development and implementation, 80–82, *98*

diagnostic assessments, 33–34, 39–41, *42*

DIBELS assessments, *102*

direct assessments, 83

duration recording, *44, 46*

equitable education, 18; and DDDM, 93–94; federal approaches to, 20–21; and MTSS, *60,* 64

equity-based relevant action research, xii, 17–31; collaboration and partnership with diverse families, 26–27; culturally

responsive, relevant, and sustaining action research, 21–23; culturally sustaining action research, 23–25, *24*; culturally sustaining evidence-based practices and interventions, 25; ensuring equity in assessment, 41–43; federal approaches to equitable education, 20–21; increasing diversity and inequitable experiences, 19–20; key takeaways, 27; key terms, 18; locating further information, *28*
equity-oriented science, 20–21
ESOL services, 101, *101*
Espin, C. A., 49
event recording, *44, 45*
Every Student Succeeds Act, 2015, xiii, 2, 12, 35, 58
evidence-based practices (EBPs), 3, 35, 59, 80, 86, 124; culturally sustaining, 25; defined, 2

families, collaboration and partnership with, 26–27, 111, 121
Family Educational Rights and Privacy Act (FERPA), 120, 130
feedback to students, 39
fidelity of implementation, 2, 20, 73, 80, 91–93; three dimensions of, 92
formal assessments, 35–36
formative assessments, 34, 39, 123
functional behavioral assessment (FBA), 34, 40–41

general education, 59
general education classroom, viii

Harrison, C., 131
high-intensity needs, 57
high-leverage practices (HLPs), 23, 26
high-quality classroom implementation with fidelity, 80, 81, 92
holistic profile of student, 26
hypothesis, 4, *6*

immigrant/refugee backgrounds, 19
implementation timeline (experiment), 4
Individualized Education Program (IEP), 57
individualized interventions, 35, 39
Individuals with Disabilities Act (IDEA), Part B, vii–viii

individual teacher action research, 10, *11*
inequities, educational, 19–20
Institute of Educational Sciences, 19, 21
institutional review board (IRB), 120, 129–30
International Literacy Association, 129
intersectionality, 18, 19–20

journals, educational, 127–28, *128*

Killion, J., 131

Ladson-Billings, Gloria, 22
latency recording, *44, 47*
lesson study, 120, 123–24
Lewin, Kurt, 7

marginalized groups or individuals, 18
minoritized groups or individuals, 18, 19
multilingual learners (MLs), 19
multiple school-based teams, vii, ix
multi-tiered system of supports (MTSS), vii, ix–x, 12, 57–71; action research (AR) using data-driven decision-making within, xiii, 97–117; action research (AR) within, 64–67, *65, 67*; and assessment data, 35, 51–53; continuous progress monitoring, 80–85, *86, 87*–88, *90, 92*; core curriculum, 58–59; defined, 2; determining student supports, *67*; and equitable education, 20–21; equity-focused framework, *59*; essential components, 59, *60*; key takeaways, 68; key terms, 57–58; locating further information, *68*–*69*; and positive behavioral interventions and supports, 58, 60; response to intervention (RtI), 58, 60; social-emotional learning (SEL), 58, 60; tiers of the MTSS framework, 61–63, 76. *See also* action research using data-driven decision-making within MTSS

National Academies of Sciences, Engineering, and Medicine, 20–21
National Center of Intensive Interventions (NCII), 110

observations, *77*; and assessment, 43–47, *43*–*47*; data collection for behavior, *44*

one-to-one and small group discussions, 39
opportunities to use and share action research within educational settings, xiii, 119–34; facilitating dialogue, 121; key takeaways, 133; key terms, 119–20; lesson study, 120, 123–24; leveraging to become educational leaders, 130–31; locating further information, *134*; presenting findings, 126–27, *127*; proactive professional development, 130–31; professional learning communities (PLCs), 119–20; professional organizations, 128–29, *129*; publishing results, 127–28, *128*; reports and presentations, 125–30, *126*; sharing and reporting action research results, 120–22; sharing data with key stakeholders, 122; sharing in professional learning communities, 122–25; sharing with profession and educational field at large, 127; using data to become educational leader and advocate, 131–33
"othering," 19

Paris, Django, 22
participatory policy approach, 26
pedagogical practices, 73
Polloway, E. A., 23
portfolio, professional, 124–25
positive behavioral interventions and supports (PBIS), 20, 40–41, 82, 110; and MTSS, 58, 60
poverty, students living in, viii, ix, 19
problem statement, 78
professional development, 130–31
professional learning communities (PLCs), 101, 119; sharing research in, 122–25
professional organizations, 128–29, *129*
progress monitoring: and assessment data, 34, *38, 42, 50*; continuous, 80–85; and DDDM, 80, 81–82; and MTSS framework, 61–63
Publication Manual of the American Psychological Association, 128
Purdue University's Online Writing Lab, 128

qualitative research, 2, 4, 6
quantitative research, 2, 4

racially, ethnically, and linguistically diverse (RELD), viii
racial or ethnic minorities, 19
reflection, *5,* 6, *6,* 14; on culturally responsive collaboration, 26–27; for culturally sustaining action research, *24*; for data collection and assessment, 53; and DDDM process, 84–85, *86,* 116; specific questions for, 8
Regional Resource Centers, 131
replacement behavior, 34, 40
research question(s), 4, *6,* 86, *86*
response to intervention (RtI), 58, 60
Rossetti, Z., 26

School Improvement Plan, 37
school-wide action research, 10, *11*
Smylie, M., 132
social-emotional learning (SEL), 58, 60
special education, 63; high-leverage practices (HLPs), 23, 26
stakeholders, 122
standardized student testing, 35–36, *38*
Standards for Excellence in Education Research, 21
summative assessment, 34, 41

target behavior, 34, 40
targeted, differentiated instruction, 12
Teacher Leadership Exploratory Consortium, 131
Teachers: accountability, 35–36; as agents of change, 7; as primary researchers, 6; systematic reflection by, *5,* 6, *6,* 8
team meetings, 84–85, 93, 104, 115
traditional research, 2, 4, *6*
triangulation, 73, 83

universal screening, 34, 37, *38, 42*
US Department of Education (USDOE), vii–viii; Institute of Educational Sciences, 21
US Department of Health and Human Services, 130

variables, 4, *6*

work sample analyses, *47,* 47–48